YOU SHOT MY SHEEP, MR. PRESIDENT

Time to Walk the Talk
From Afghanistan to New York

William Kornfeld

© William Kornfeld 2013

You shot my sheep, Mr President

Published by William Kornfeld
P.O.Box 13152, Nelspruit, Riverside 1226, Mpumalanga
William.Kornfeld@yahoo.com

ISBN 978-0-620-59144-7

All rights reserved. No part of this publication may be reproduced, stored in a retrieval system, or transmitted in any form by any means electronic, mechanical, photocopying, recording or otherwise without the written permission of the copyright owner.

This is a work of fiction. Names, characters, businesses, places, events and incidents are either the products of the author's imagination or are used in a fictitious manner. Any resemblance to actual persons, living or dead, or actual events is purely coincidental, and there is no inference that actual persons would behave in the manner that the author has had them behave.

Layout by Boutique Books

For the President

INTRODUCTION

Two young men, a German world traveller and an Afghan shepherd, who have been brought up in two different worlds, in different religions and cultures, under extremely different life circumstances, become friends in the war zone of the Afghanistan desert. They exchange their life stories and dreams – dreams they want to live, dreams they can't afford – and they find out together that they would do nearly anything to have their dreams come true.

An adventurous plan develops to get the finance for the fulfilment of their dreams. The plan sounds like a crazy action movie, including an impressive plot which won't harm any people... but which will be a wake-up call to those who are in power to change the future and to end wars.

When an awful massacre happens in close proximity to the two friends, they leave the desert to turn the plan into reality, all depending on which interest group, during this crazy war, decides to pay them... to do... or not to do... what they planned!

So they go... and start to Walk the Talk, delivering a unique message to the world, and to the President of the United States of America.

CONTENTS

	Page
Introduction	5
Contents	7
Desert Friendship	9
Not Only A Book	23
The Plan Of Action	33
Time To Go	57
Bangkok	66
Jambo Africa	80
Into Mozambique	95
Beira, Boat And Mines	105
Boat And Tower Building	123
Around Africa's Coast	136
Trans Atlantic	147
The Final Countdown	163
Firework With A Message	175
An Act Of God	184
Author's Note	192

DESERT FRIENDSHIP

There is a terrible smell of goats and sheep, and their excrement, mixed into the smoke of our camp fire. Sometimes there is a slight draft of grenade explosions, and gun shots, far back in the mountains, but otherwise it is a peaceful spot under a clear sky in the Afghanistan desert.

Close to me I hear the newest pop songs and America's nightlife is passing by my eyes at a hurried speed... he, Harun, is staring at the little screen of his iPad, which he found close to an accident scene, and which he'd taken away from an American soldier after a deadly car crash.

Hollywood... New York... Miami beach and its flipping Bikini Girls... Las Vegas, super cars and bikes, dream homes: the whole American dream, out of a little high-tech device, which seems to have the whole world filed. His eyes are staring at that little screen, eating and inhaling the pictures and documentation he is shown. He just can't believe what he sees, and he can't get enough of it. Harun is focused on the little screen of his iPad like there is no war around him.

I've known him for nearly four weeks now, and I am still impressed with his English knowledge. He said he got taught it in order to understand the enemy, and has nothing else to do other than learn the language while he cares all day for his goats and sheep. He just learned with old books and had hardly any opportunity to practise, so his pronunciation is even stranger than my English, me being German-born but living in South Africa.

I asked him who the enemy is. He said, "America!"

And I asked him what he knows about America? He said that it is the most powerful and biggest country, with Presidents that like to make war. But, as he sees now on his iPad, it is also one of the most beautiful countries, with a high and luxurious lifestyle, and is not only a dream world.

He asks, "Why do their Presidents not look after their own country, on their own soil? Don't they have enough to do there, in such a huge country?" He makes me smile and I tell him about the United States' history, that they started out as thirteen small and vulnerable colonies clinging to the east coast of North America. Over the next century, those original thirteen states expanded all the way across the continent, subjugating or exterminating the native population and wresting Texas, New Mexico, Arizona and California from Mexico.

I told him that they had fought a bitter civil war, had acquired a modest set of overseas colonies, and had come late to both world wars. But, since becoming a great power in around 1900, the United States have fought nearly a dozen genuine wars and engaged in countless military interventions outside their country. In Vietnam, thirteen million people got killed, mostly civilians. This nearly outdid Hitler's disastrous war, but no one talks about that anymore.

I told him that I believe that if they had kept their dirty, bloody, dollar-crooked fingers out of the business of these nations, these countries, so full of depressed, exploited people, would have arrived at a solution of their own – one that they'd designed and wanted, that they'd fought and worked for – and not the American style and footprint, which they don't want.

I don't believe they had any rights to invade a foreign country, not even under the given reasons of needing to sort out their politics, religion, economic structures and cultural issues.

The years of colonization are over. Strange, they do not care about the Congo, or Zimbabwe. Is it maybe because there is no oil? Just human beings in our time when the world is totally over populated?

Harun and I have shared plenty of late evenings here already, sitting under the most beautiful sky of stars, in the middle of the Afghanistan desert, discussing all kind of issues in this world. I am the one who is usually talking, being the one who has got more to tell, and the one who has got an answer to nearly each of his endless questions. For me it seems like teaching how to live life to someone who had always been locked up and had never experienced the real world.

I lived and experienced it all over again in this beautiful, exciting world, where I travelled and worked, while he was guarding his goats and sheep in this laid back Afghanistan desert.

"So William, do you think something like that really exists? Is it all real? All this wealth and luxury and these wonderful things?" he asks me, while pointing at pictures of fascinating dream homes, with crystal-clear pools, expensive sports cars, and barely-dressed models on beautiful beaches.

I turn my head, to look into his eyes to see if he is joking, but the look in these so-innocent eyes of this now thirty-two-year-old Afghan shepherd seem to be serious. He repeats his question. "Come on, tell me. You said you have been all over the world!"

I say, "Yes, that's real, and, well, you haven't seen anything yet. This world's got a billion faces and locations, people and situations. It's all out there, and it's real, fast and dangerous, but exciting and enjoyable too! One just needs lots of money, and one needs to know how to live life and how to set priorities for oneself!

"Yes, I saw a lot of it, some very close, in real, some passing by, some only from far away, on a screen as you do now, but I never had the money to really live the luxury, up-market lifestyle myself, even as close as I was to it. To check into a five-star hotel or buy a dream car or even a dream home, that kind of cash I never had.

"I had a fantastic childhood, raised in a little village in Germany, and I travelled Europe with the wildest tribe of boy scouts in my teenage years, singing in the streets, and giving blood in hospitals to have pocket money. Then there were four adventurous years in the paratroops in the German army, before I sailed to South America.

I was in and out there for four years, working in tourism. Then I spent thirteen years in Southern Africa, and nearly two years in Thailand, and now I am here in the Afghanistan desert during a damn useless war, which hopefully won't harm me. I am only here because of the money I am paid for working here. I will never earn a higher salary back home.

"I always lived very basically, on little salary, and just enjoyed working and living surrounded by nature and a beautiful paradise under Africa's sun, but cash was always short. I could hardly afford to attend my best friend's birthday parties or wedding. Nor was I able to visit my dad for his seventieth birthday. The few cars I owned were more than twenty years old and just got me from A to B when necessary. But I always lived healthily, did lots of outdoor activities, had lots of beautiful girlfriends and love affairs, and I guess that kept me young.

"I will never give up my dreams. Life can be beautiful, and one doesn't need that much, but I still need a little more than I can ever earn with my odd jobs. Dreams are important to stay positive and to have a goal and a destiny in life. People who don't have dreams do not live."

"So why don't you go back home and earn more money?"

"I am on my way there with the money I earn here, doing this dangerous job, and should be able to start a business back home in South Africa. I hope and believe that in five years, when I am fifty, I will be able to go out and just live life to the fullest, start the business and be my own boss. Yes, life is expensive – and the good life is even more expensive. A life that is only full off fun and pleasure is damn expensive.

"If you are rich, you have to watch out who your friends are. At the moment, being poor, I know that all my friendships are real and genuine. And my friends love me just for the person I am."

"Oh, hahaha," he laughs. "Till you are rich! You are an old man!"

"Yey.. hey... shut up!" I shout at him that all I want is to be free, and to be living in the countryside, enjoying nature and the basics of a good life, and to have time to dream, and to be artistic and creative, in my little workshop, and in my kitchen, and to write my adventures and dreams in books, and to share them with others.

"You are lucky! You can sit here most of the day with your goats and sheep, in this beautiful country. Yes, okay, at this time you have a war around you, but at least you are free in your little world, and have beautiful scenery here and you can dream and do all day what you want. Damn, you could write books all day!"

He turns his head, looking at me, nearly cross, but I see also that his eyes are getting wet and then he nearly cries, "I am sitting here with the goats since I am four years old. First with my Uncle, till I was eleven. Then he got too old to come out with me, so the last twenty years, I sit here alone, day for day. Now, you tell me, what shall I write about? How to look after goats and sheep in the Afghanistan desert? I can write it in five minutes... but nobody wants to read that anyway!

"I haven't lived, I haven't experienced anything exciting of this world. I never sat in a car, and I never had a girlfriend. The effect of so-called alcohol sounds like a fairytale to me. At the moment, I wouldn't know how my life will ever change!

"You, you lived, experienced and survived interesting adventures and countries. You lived and love to write your life in books. This is what I know about you so far and I am already so jealous.

"Can't you take me out of here? Can't we just go, and do something, do something exciting and experience the real life?"

"Gossshhh, my boy, I am with you. I understand where you're coming from. A whole life in a desert, and you might have never known different, if you hadn't found this iPad. Now it makes you unhappy, unfulfilled. I understand very well how you must feel! The poorest people in Africa don't have a fridge or a bed, but they have a damn TV, which screws up their mind too!

"For sure, you want to get out into the world and see, and live, just as I want to, hey?"

We've got something big in common. We share a big dream of freedom and adventure and independence and fun in the sun. And we bang our hands against each other: high five!

This I taught him in the first days when we met here, the afternoon I had been left at the market in Mazar, without getting any meat for my tented kitchen outside town. Oh yes, it is so typically me to take on a crazy catering job in Afghanistan, but I don't deserve any better. I begged for it, and I got it.

With a smile, I remember the scene in my office, an admin job in Cape Town. Once again, I lost my temper there and nearly hit, with my flat hand, the screen at my workplace – and I screamed at my supervisor, "Damn shit job here! I'd be better off going off to war, to shoot for money – or even getting shot! That would still be better than dying here little by little each minute, solving the idiotic peanuts problems of spoiled and stupid clients. Here I feel more used and abused than I would in a real-life war zone!"

The next day I had just had my second coffee of the morning when the local recruitment agency called me.

"Hi, William, I think that this time we've got a job made for you!"

I started smiling, and asked what it was all about.

"Well, it's a catering job, quite a challenge but very well paid!"

"How much?" was my immediate question.

"Five thousand Euro a month," came the answer!

"Waaoouuwww, but where is the hook? There is nothing like that in South Africa…or in Africa?"

"No, there isn't, and it is much further away!"
"Where?"
"It is close to Mazar."
"To where?"
"Well... south east of Kabul."
"In Afghanistan?" I repeat.
"Yes, William, in Afghanistan. It is for a Saudi-Arabian company, based in Dubai, with German management. They want a third world experienced caterer, and the job will be in a tented kitchen, making three meals a day for up to two hundred men."
"Men only?"
"Yes, construction workers building new streets, highways, airports in Afghanistan. You will have a team of ten helpers. The challenge is the food supply. You need to organize the supply from the local market."
"Well, it sounds interesting, but as far I know there are no bottle stores, or life-saving Mc Donalds close by?"
"Nooo!" came the amused reply.
"This income could get me out of my hole... but it's dangerous too!"
"Well, William, think about it. I know it's something quite different, but I believe you've got the right experience to do it. And you are German!"

So I thought it over for a night, and applied. Then I had a few Skype interviews with German people I have never seen, and, to make a long story short, once again my life turned into a movie, as I departed on Emirates Airline, not even a week later. I met my bosses in Dubai, in a fancy air-conditioned office, and stayed five days in a luxury, five-star hotel, while we bought and ordered all kinds of equipment to be sent to Afghanistan. Nice. They even set up a high life insurance for me, benefiting my younger brother and older sister, in case the shit hit my fan.

The personal weapon I asked for was denied. They said that I'd be a caterer there, not a soldier. "Well, let me just get there," I thought.

As we landed in a freight carrier in Kabul my usual question came up in mind. "When will I ever leave here again? How will life change from here?"

It was dry and dusty, as I knew the climate in Namibia to be. We loaded our stuff on three trucks and hit the road; lovely scenery, but too much military presence all over, at each crossing and turn off. Well, it's a war zone, not to forget.

Then we built up four tents in total, connected to a bombed-out house, where we got the water supply and power for a cooling container. That was already much more infrastructure than I'd expected, and my memories of living in the Amazon, twenty years ago, woke up. The only running water there was the river Rio Caura, and electricity became available only after a few months, when I installed a one-cylinder generator for the evening hours. The good old days.

The first weeks in Afghanistan seemed to be easy, since we'd also imported quite a supply of food. This gave me time to discover the local markets, and to secure a further and regular supply.

And, after a few days, a routine set in. Most of my helpers spoke not one word of anything near to English, so it was like it always is in the third world: showing with hands, giving the different activities short easy words to remember – like cut; wash; clean – so they learned them quickly. And they learned very fast that, if I had to repeat an instruction by getting slightly louder, then they had to work faster and better, learning by doing as we say. I might be harsh sometimes, but that gives me the talent to make things clear with a few words only!

Luckily, this was not an *a la carte* restaurant, so the workers had to eat whatever I cooked. There was no alternative, and no tip money to expect either.

So here are Harun and me sitting again at the camp fire, like every evening, instead of going to a local pub or beach bar like at home in Cape Town. Here I grab the rusty old Land Rover, and chase down the dirt road for half an hour, passing four checkpoints, chatting to various nations of military personnel, all of them bored to death and with a question mark over their face: what the hell are they actually doing here?

This has become my routine evening activity, after I have fed my worker crowd with some self-designed food, which I created using the ingredients given and available. The workers seem happy – well, I like what I cook – and there is always enough for a second helping. And with Harun as my local friend, food supply has got better, with daily meat – "free range goats and lamb" – which I cook as curry, stir fry and even sometimes on a *spitbraai*.

Occasionally, I feel very tired and bored of it, and I feel like going to a cosy, busy pub for a good, cold beer, or to a good South African barbecue with red wine. Then I mingle with the American or German soldiers and have access to their beer supply, and we discuss the nonsense of this war, which, considering the way it has been going for nearly ten years, might never end.

These soldiers do not even feel like soldiers, but like police or security personnel. Even so, they get ambushed and killed here. What kind of war is that, where you cannot see the enemy and no direction is given as to where to go, where to fight? And, if you defend yourself, you might end up in court and you have to justify anything you did by following orders from officers who don't have a clue about what they are doing here. The press and media usually take the opportunity to turn stories around, and publish them to the outside world, turning the facts around as well as they can, making out of a small incident a huge catastrophe before the highly decorated generals and diplomats in charge can comment upon the situation, or decide whose fault it was that the last attack or fight has cost casualties, even for the civilians.

Wars always have casualties, that's what comes with it, and one has to deal with where it happens, and everybody involved in wars should know that.

Now I stare into the fire and get stuck in my dreams, drinking undefined tea and discussing with and explaining to an Afghan shepherd all the world's problems and issues, the economy and politics.

Harun always wakes me out of my daydreams.

"Hey, William, please let's go!"

"Let's go? Where to? How? Oh, my boy... I wish it could be that easy. I got here with my last thousand Rand – that's about a hundred and forty US dollars – and you? How many million dollars have you saved? Shepping for twenty years, without beering and girling?"

Oh shit, now I've hit his weakest point. Shit, my sarcasm will kill me one day. He throws a piece of burning wood after me; it misses my face by half an inch. I turn my head, but don't say a word. Now, for the first time, I don't see the face of a shepherd, I see a man's face, the face of a man who looks like he's locked up in a cage, but has the determined desire to break out!

I apologize and he looks at me and says, "Next time I kill you!"

Now my eyes open wide and I ask, "What?"

He repeats in his really funny English, "Yes, you understood. If you talk that bad shit, I kill you! I don't want you as friend... then you must go... then you are not a friend... and then I don't care if you are dead!"

Uusshhhhh, I get the message and understand the aggression. Don't tickle a lion in a cage. I bend over and apologize again. I go on my knees and stay down with my face to the ground. It takes a while – well seconds can sometimes feel like hours – and then he just throws a handful of goat shit at me and starts laughing. Well, I have nothing else to do, other than join in, and we are friends again, laughing and jumping around the fire in the bloody middle of nowhere! We are enjoying a special friendship between two strong-minded men, who've got stuck in the mud.

When we sit down again, he looks at me very seriously and he says, "William, you are my only friend, and my life got already different since I met you. Now, let's make plans. What, how can we do, to live our dreams, to live a better life?"

Gosh, with his young, innocent, but demanding look on his sun burned face, I feel that, for the first time, I've met someone with the same desire as I have, ready to do anything to get a different life. He's really done more than his duty, twenty years looking after goats. I had more than twenty years looking after tourists, and the difference is most of the time not that big. Same basic scenario: taking care that they don't get sun burned, and always having cold drinks available, feeding them nicely and putting them to bed. That's how you keep tourists – and goats – happy. Sadly, I wasn't allowed to kick the tourists or throw a stone at them to keep them quiet.

"Yes, my friend," I say, "I am glad we can sit here... dream and plan... and, if we get the right plan, I am more than ready to turn this plan into reality, trust me with that!

"I feel as young as you, full of spirit and power! And, of course I have had these dreams since I could think, always dreaming of the lottery jackpot win, or the big deal. It drives me nuts what a Formula One driver earns, what a professional soccer player earns, what a movie star cashes in, and what a life they live. But they are just a few lucky ones!

"And I like to imagine having a huge amount, like a jackpot in the lottery, and to go house and car shopping, setting up my own little world, self-designed and equipped, my own space, where my friends can come and go as they wish!

"A little farm in Africa, with a fresh-water pond, self-sufficient. And to finally meet the right wife, who can cook as well as I can. She does not have to skin grapes for me, but if she can drink whiskey, and make my steaks medium rare, then she might be the one.

"It is a huge dream, doing every day only that which you feel like doing, having the peace and freedom and cash to live a dream life. By now I am ready to do anything for a big amount, once off. Yes, I am ready, even for something a bit out of the normal run of things."

"What you mean?" he asks.

"Well, I am only watching and observing this stupid war, and all the bullshit talk they come up with about it, sometimes in the news or in the newspaper, and listening how many million, well, billion, dollars it costs. And for what? Only for more trouble, more death and suffering. I believe there are easier ways to prove power, to set signs, to get heard, to change things. Yes, there are. And now that I've witnessed all this waste with my own eyes every day, it makes me think even more, and more deeply, about how to get some attention – or maybe even give advice about how to change things.

"These presidents of the big nations – especially of the United States –have to learn that they cannot abuse their power in foreign territories and cultures. They must learn, learn a lesson, that arguing with monstrous weapons and fighter planes belongs to the past. It is no solution at all, to destroy the other parties' property and infrastructure, just to get some bad people, or a dictator, to justice. They've lost total control of the main issue, they get controlled by scurrilous money-makers and industries. A war is just not the right tool for resolving issues anymore. It's got too expensive and too much unforgettable damage gets done without solving the problem. Haven't they learned from the crazy world wars we've had?

"But where and how will a President learn? What education do these Presidents bring with them to get so much power?

"Oh, I love to remember a joke, where one of those presidents took his wife incognito to a five-star restaurant, to have a romantic evening. There the wife is approached by the manager and told that the owner wishes to speak to her for a minute. Well, she gets up and does him the favour because she's recognized him as one of her school-time lovers, and they have a little chat. Back at the dinner table she tells her husband about the meeting. He says, 'Oh, dear, if you had married him, then you would have a husband with a lovely five-star restaurant.'

"'No, my love,' she says, 'then he would be the President!'

"It seems that the US Presidents are still like the cowboys of a hundred years ago. If they have a strong, fast horse and a revolver they think they can do anything in their own interest. But, with all due respect, their military actions in Iraq and Afghanistan are not wars, and ought not to be called wars. They are occupations.

"Calling them 'wars' gives them undue moral weight, and helps continue them indefinitely, to the profit of their arms industry and at the expense of their nation's taxpayers. And since wars must be won or lost, the 'wars' in Iraq and Afghanistan can never end, because they don't have an enemy to defeat."

These are quite some issues to discuss with an Afghan shepherd, but any halfway intelligent human will understand it.

"Politicians are different. They are only puppets of their nation industries, while they get overrun by the media. Occupations can only be ended – they are not won – and to end a ten-year-long mistake, it takes the character, strength and balls of a highly intelligent leader, which seems not to be found anymore!

"In 2008, Americans elected Barack Obama in part because they thought he would be different from his predecessor on a host of issues, but especially in his approach to the use of armed force. It was clear to nearly everyone that George W. Bush had launched a foolish and unnecessary war in Iraq, and then compounded the error by mismanaging it. And as if that mistake was not enough, he went even further and started another war in Afghanistan.

"So, Americans chose a candidate who had opposed Bush's war in Iraq and could bring U.S. commitments back in line with our resources. Above all, Americans thought Obama would be a lot more thoughtful about where and how to use force, and that he understood the limits of this crudest of policy tools. The Norwegian Nobel Committee seems to have thought so too, when they awarded him the Nobel Peace Prize, not for anything he had done, but for what it hoped he might do in the future.

"Seems he never got the message and it is time he gets a clearer one, I think!

"South Africa, with its former President Nelson Mandela, is the best example in history of how a whole country can change, through negotiation, convincing talks and patience, not through war and with weapons, but through one single, highly intelligent, demanding man!

"The end of apartheid in South Africa, and the end of the wall between west and east Germany, are the only two bloodless revolutions in world history, and they were so because their people kept together. They were strong, and never gave up, and they did not want war or oil, only peace, through sharing and mixing what they had, and who they were.

"They demanded their rights, and got them!"

NOT ONLY A BOOK

"So what are you trying to tell me?" Harun asks. "What are you thinking of? What do you mean? What?"

"Hey, *boytjie*, I am talking about writing a book, which will hopefully be turned into a movie! A story that is understandable to everybody, not only the so-called highly educated politicians who talk themselves stupid and spin issues upside-down.

"I'm thinking about a clever kind of attack – or, better, let's call it a plot – that is very different from others, but which is just supposed to become a movie to remind the world once again that wars do not make, and have never made, sense. War always hits the innocents, are a waste of money – a pure waste, especially while millions of people are hungry, and don't even have water and shelter. Today, where everybody thinks he is highly educated and knows everything, and gets answers from the internet anywhere – just as you do on your iPad – even more and much bigger mistakes are made in the world than were ever made in world history before!

"It's a stupid arrogant power play by big politicians, the mafia, investment schemes and industries, who all benefit from wars, but the world's people pay for it, and get nothing out except for suffering and sadness.

"What this Afghanistan war costs per day could feed tens of millions of people each day, but who thinks about that?

"Humans are like ants. They keep on moving and multiplying even though I really don't understand anymore how they master their daily lives in a lot of countries. So many just exist with much less than the basics, under the hardest conditions one can imagine.

"So, maybe with a movie that hits millions of viewers with its hidden story and which has a clear message for everybody in it, can help to start changing people's minds and get them back on track about how to make it a better world for all. The people need to wake up and keep together and go out on the street and demonstrate. Do something more than just swearing in front of their TV on their cosy couch!

"It is high time to stop useless wars. The world leaders need to combine what they've got and share it and stop using each other. It's all about a big wake up call, but some seem never to wake up. Now the whole of Europe wants to stop nuclear power stations, and they all go for sun power. And they make the biggest problem again about the money, who pays who for the sun? They bicker about how much needs to be paid for sunlight, which is given by nature.

"Where is the most sun? Well, in Africa, where people starve because there is no water and food. So why not just help each other by exchanging what each party has and needs. Water supports farming and food supply, sun gives electricity for the first world's toys. Every child in at school could make a plan for that!

"Sun for water! Why dig for dirty oil, when the sun rises every day for all of us!

"It is not reinventing the wheel, it is all about sharing what's given.

"Give water for sun! Not bullets for oil!

"I'd love to distribute the message with my book or movie to millions all over the world. I'd like to put my creative energy into a story full of adventures and fun, while fulfilling a huge mission: delivering a clear message, one that cannot be misunderstood, to make people stand up and think that wars are not a tool for intelligent people.

"President Bush called for a war against terror!

"That's like trying to kill all mosquitoes in the Amazon, because a few of them will bite you one day!

"I might be a slave of my lively fantasy, but I also know that it all will make sense, and it is worth a try, and here I've got the time and peace after work, away from the dazzle of nightlife and temptations of a western city."

"Hey! Hey, what you talking? What you got in mind?" the shepherd asks and he is getting more and more curious by the minute, and with each word I share with him.

"I can see an action, a plot, how something gets done to the most powerful by some unknown, adventures guys, something that wakes the world powers, that would show them that there are other ways of doing things. A wakeup call to look at the world's problems from a different angle and find better and fairer solutions to make this a better world, not by killing and long stupid wars, but by using our brains and wisdom!

"We haven't inherited this planet from our ancestors, we've borrowed it from our children! And we cannot make our children pay for our generation's mistakes.

"Please do not misunderstand me. I am not a terrorist!

"No! No, all I want is to write a book, and try to make a movie, so that as many people as possible all over the world will get the message and start thinking again."

Harun looks at me, and I can see the steam in his brain boiling up.

His eyes are looking for some seconds into my left eye, and then some seconds into my right eye, as if he is trying to x-ray my brain. Then he asks, very soft and thoughtfully, "But, if they, I mean if nobody likes buying and reading your book, or nobody wants to produce the movie? Or if nobody is interested in reading or watching? How do you know that someone will pay you for your story and that they pay you enough and fair? If they rip you off like other industries do, what then?

"Sometimes I have the fattest goats and sheep, and nobody likes to buy them! Are you sure it's a perfect plan in your book, and it would work in real?"

"Yes, I believe so. I've thought about it a lot of times, when I've watched primitive American action movies, and I've got a creative adventure fantasy. It's going to be quite a long way to go, lots of complications, but nothing that couldn't be done. A challenge beyond your fantasy, enough to fill plenty of books which can be written afterwards.

"Yes, it will work. It will be dangerous, but it will work!"

"Okay," he says, "if you are really sure, then I know the people that pay you to do so!"

"What do you mean?" I ask.

He says, "Well, if you know how to do big damage to the enemy, how you can scare him, how to prove he is vulnerable, I am sure you will get paid from my people!"

I look at him, speechless. I've never thought of really turning my fantasy idea into action. Neither have I really thought of supporting any party in this war. It is not my war, although whose war is it? Everybody's war? We all live on and from this planet earth, which isn't made better by wars, and we all have to share the consequences!

He interrupts my silence, by asking again, "William, do you really think you can do that kind of damage to America?"

Now he makes me think. The playful action story I had in mind for my book can be turned into reality. Yes, it can be. It would be dangerous, but possible!

"So what, German?" He calls me that the first time. "Can you? Or can you not?"

I see a sprinkling of stars in his dark brown eyes. He is caught by the idea, can imagine doing something for his country and people and being part of something big. I can read it in his eyes.

"My dear friend Harun, YES, my plan can work in reality. But it will be quite a job, and there are only you and me to do it!"

Now his frozen look turns into a smile. "Tell me what I need to do?"

"Oh, slowly. Slowly! There is no rush. A good plan is ninety percent of the success, but my plans all fall down because of the same stupid reason!"

"What? Why?" he screams.

"We need some cash. Unreasonably little for what we will achieve, but we need some capital. There is quite something to be built, and a looooong way to go."

He hunches down, staring into the fire, not saying a word, looking like his only hope got demolished in one sentence.

"It is late already. Okay, let's think about all of it. There are lots of thoughts and information to share between us. Luckily, we've got plenty of time. There's no reason for any hurry. And don't you dare talk to anyone about it. So far it is an idea – a very, very, veerrryy dangerous idea, but nobody out there has even to know that we've got thoughts like this. Promise you won't talk to anyone, not even to your goats!"

"I promise by Allah! Whatever. But, please tell me more about your idea and plan!"

"Look, the last official education I had was in the army in Germany in the late eighties, and that was during a kind of peace, the so called 'cold war', and I have never been in combat, but I am highly educated in explosives and sabotage, and I still do know how to handle all kinds of explosives and to build bombs, hidden bombs, tricky bombs. Very basic, but very, very powerful. One doesn't need to highjack planes and crash with innocent people into a sky scraper.

"I believe there is an easier way, a way even more impressive, and now that I am nearly an old man, as you say, I am ready to do something, something unique, something the world will look at and could benefit from. And if it helps us to live our dream life, if someone pays me, I mean *us*, to do it in their interests, and we don't kill anybody, just give an impressive demonstration, or let's call it 'giving a wake up call or a message by blowing out a big candle' – yes, that is a nice way to put it – then all the better. But please, don't ask for further details yet."

"Why not? Please tell me about your idea!" he screams.

"Hey, cool down my friend, this is a big thing we've brought up here, a huge thing, which might change our lives forever, and that makes my brain steam, with thousands of thoughts crossing my mind. I need a serious drink now, so I'd better go back to my container. I need some quiet time to think.

"My dear friend, Harun, Let's sleep on what we've discussed now. It is quite something, and won't be easy going, but it might be our only way to make, sooner or later, our dreams into reality.

"You have as little to lose as I have, and that's a good basis for a team of two! Good night, my friend. Get your sleep and rest. See you tomorrow!"

The next day I cook horrible food. My mind is somewhere else, far away from this duty of this desert kitchen, and this crowd of workers that I've got to feed. They are a herd of goats in clothes for me, nothing else, and they mumble strange languages of which I don't understand a word. In a week's time it will be the second pay-day, five thousand Euro, and that is another fifty thousand South African Rand. In the last fifteen years I've never owned such an amount. It is a lot of money for me, for a gypsy, and it could keep me going for quite a while, but it is not enough to get a business started, so once again I have to kick my ass myself and hang in there, maybe for another month. Yes, that gives me a month's worth of time to really think and discuss possibilities.

I start to love the evenings at the fire even more. They are very strange evenings, with no beer or wine, just tea. I've no cigarettes anymore, and girls... gosshh, I've nearly forgotten what they look like! Shame!

One day I am early at the goat and sheep camp. I love driving the dusty country roads, overtaking military convoys which are wasting fuel and manpower moving from nowhere to nowhere.

They've been sent by their governments, and are following orders from inexperienced officers and stubborn diplomats without uniforms, who only count the days before they can go home again.

All manpower, and even femalepower these days, and all the materials sent here by various world powers, will never be enough to conquer this land and its people. There is no way to change these strong believers. All these soldiers and materials are only sent here for the media to make the world powers look good, as if something is being done.

The media is one of the primary benefiters of these wars. They use TV and internet to show the whole world about all the combat around the world in five minutes.

People have fought each other since forever, for thousands of years, but only since the media got so powerful do we know about all the horrible events, as they happen.

These soldiers in high tech uniforms and armed with modern equipment, are just toys of war. If they are lucky they'll get home alive, and with the good salaries they get for serving in a war zone, they might be able to pay off a house, or take their families on dream vacations, but too many of them have got killed already, albeit in relatively small numbers when compared with other wars. Nevertheless, it is still enough to fill the news and steer the first world's population into supporting this useless war, for there are still those who believe this manipulating media of today.

And, even with all the coverage, I really don't know enough details about this crazy, useless war, which has already taken too long, too many years. The Russians and the English had to learn a hard and expensive lesson before in Afghanistan, and now the Americans and their alliances think they can do better.

I guess that most people don't know what it is all about anymore. Me neither. The reasons that it all started are nearly forgotten, it has just been going on too long already. And nobody's really got a serious plan about how to finish it. Or it might be better to say that nobody's got the balls to stop the shit that's going on here!

I am glad that I am a civilian out here, with all kinds of security proof hanging around my neck, and am able to pass all checkpoints and road blocks.

And yes, I've made friends with lots of them, knowing they have beer in their camps. I always get my beer, even where it's not really available! And I got the U.S. code for the internet here, and this is what keeps Harun on his iPad-toy, which is opening up the outside world for him in digital format.

This evening, when I get to the camp, Harun has just put a goat on a spit over the fire. He usually only makes this once a month, so I am surprised and positively impressed and thank him for the effort.

"Let us celebrate that we will make a plan, and start a new life," he shouts.

He says he bought the goat, she is not from his herd, so he doesn't know if it's going to be as delicious.

"You bought the goat? With what money?" I ask him and he tells me that the dead soldier, on whom he found the iPad, had had some little cash in his purse, just enough for a goat.

"So, you stole the money from a dead American soldier? You should not steal, isn't it?"

"No. No," he says "I didn't steal it, I borrowed it. I will give it back, when we have made our job."

Fair enough, whatever, what can I say? I shake my head in this case and leave any further argument, enjoying the smell of the meat and the thought of the feast to come.

I sit down, close to him at the fire, trying to show him something on his iPad, but he holds something different in his hands: the soldier's purse with his passport, and, oh dear, pictures of someone who is probably his girlfriend,..or his girlfriends…

"No more money," Harun says, and wants to throw the purse into the fire, but I see more, and grab it out of his hands just in time and open it again. Yes, no more money, but credit cards, all the way through; a golden American Express, a Visa and a Diners Club.

I take them out and show them to Harun. Look at that!

"That looks boring," he says. Obviously he doesn't know what they are. Well, how would he?

"Listen my friend, this is nearly as good as money. Not, of course, out here in the desert, but back in the real world it could be a lot of money!"

The dead soldier was a major, so if he had been here long enough, he should have some good savings in his account – and, yes, we will give it back later.

"Explain it to me! What is it," he screams.

"Okay. Look. These are so-called credit cards, where each belongs to a bank account, which is most probably in the United States. That's where these soldiers get their salaries paid, even while they serve here."

"Oh, shit," he says. "How we get to America to the bank?"

Oh gosh, this boy knows how to make me laugh, but after yesterday's experience I will never laugh or be sarcastic when he asks something. I thought about it last night before I went to sleep. I am worlds ahead of him with my knowledge and experience, and I cannot blame him for that, but now we share a big dream.

But, to get something done together with him, I am going to need to explain a lot!

I show the cards to him, and explain some details, that there is a magnetic stripe that is needed to use cards at bank machines, to draw cash, usually possible in the whole world. The question is, where here, in the war zone in Afghanistan?

I tell him that we need their pin codes, which usually every card holder hides somewhere, but there are no notes in the purse, no written info at all. Shit. Oh well, let's wait and see.

"Please, can I have a look at his iPad?" I ask.

Now he looks at me, really scared. I know that this device is the biggest treasure he's ever had. This little thing has shown him this world in pictures. It is the fault of this device that this young man, shepherd or not, is ready to change his life, whatever it costs. Obviously, he doesn't really know how to handle it. So far he has only opened the files on the desktop, movies and pics. Well, that seems to be what the soldier had used the most, besides Google and Facebook. Now, Harun Googles all day long, and is having enormous fun with the internet.

Harun doesn't want to hand it to me. Well, so no more recharging in my kitchen then. On understanding that he hands it over to me, but he won't take his eyes off it. Now these eyes get even bigger as I open files with pics and movies he hadn't found yet. But that wasn't what I was looking for. Okay, there it is; a private address book, but with nothing filed under credit card. Damn, shit, what now?

I explain the problem to him, which takes a while, and afterwards he looks as helpless to me as before. I am not surprised. My eyes scroll over the address book, and then, Matthew Diner catches my eyes, and he's got four digits printed boldly in the telephone number field.

Hey, hey, there we go. Together with Margerethe Visa and Paul Amex, I believe I have found all three four-digit codes for all the credit cards, but where to prove if it works, where? And how to get the cash in this sandy desert area. I will find a way, maybe by purchasing something online, but that might wake up suspicions.

Here it won't help to draw local currency, if that is even possible, and it would be much too dangerous anyway.

THE PLAN OF ACTION

My mind is spinning plans. This boy would first need a passport, because we will have to do quite some travelling. A passport I will get for him in Thailand's capital, Bangkok. There I've got all kinds of contacts and connections, since I worked there before for nearly two years. I've lots of nice memories, and an active bank account too, where I even hide the salaries I earn here, unknown to the sharks of South African financial institutions.

In Thailand there are plenty of opportunities to clean out the credit cards and to exchange for hard currency. That's again where my German passport comes in handy. Okay, that's a plan for that so far. But before I share any details with Harun I need to put in further thought. At this point it is a just a too-crazy idea and plan, but damn, how I do like it! It's the kind of job made for me, where I can use all my talents. I need to keep him quiet and under self-control, knowing he will do anything to experience life with fun and pleasure. And damn, yes, he will get lots of fun when we are on our way. The fun is what I owe him. Work hard – play hard.

Whether we will we succeed in our mission is a totally different question, but haven't I been taught that there are no problems, only difficult and easy jobs, and that one is either too lazy or too stupid to do it? We are not lazy, and not stupid!

He asks me where my mind is and I tell him that I am thinking, and that everything needs to be planned very, very carefully, and that he is safer the less he knows. He says, not to worry, he can take care of himself. Yes sure, here in the desert, from the mountains to the river and back to town where he knows every little rock, but what about Bangkok, or later in Africa or even in the United States?

I tell him that he needs to promise me to do as I tell him, whatever it will be. I say that he has to trust me, because it is a huge, dangerous world out there, with very strange and dangerous people. I calm him down by confirming that he is clever and strong, and that he will learn on our way, and, if we succeed, he can then decide what he wants to do.

But first I will introduce him to this outside world. And it will be at least another two months, if we are really going to do it.

"We will," he shouts. "We must do it!"

"Yes, sure. Patience. No panic. Slowly but surely, my friend."

Somehow he is, and will be for a long time, like a child at my side, but I've had that before, in the army, when I had to make soldiers out of spoilt young men. We broke them, and then built them up as new human beings, ready to follow orders without questioning.

Using my know-how and technical knowledge, we can bring our vision to reality. I won't share with him in detail, he will learn it while doing. It is easier to show than to explain. So, it is totally up to me to plan any detail and foresee any possible problem that could occur. I like planning, we Germans are good at it. Well, I do know; I am German. And for this venture all my life experience will help, all connections will get used,

Yes, I can't stop the smile on my face, when thinking through the rough plan.

There is, however, that one issue that always follows me: the good old finance problem! I will have around fifteen thousand Euro saved when we leave here, plus the hope of at least ten thousand US dollars from the credit cards – or even more?

Or nothing? That's possible too!

Oh, oh, oh, my old favourite problem, the fucking money. Harun won't be able to add a single cent and there's nobody else who could finance us... or?

"Hey, Harun, when you say your people would pay us for such action, who will it really be? Who can we get involved with up front? Who can we – or who can *you* – trust?

"I am a bit scared, please don't understand me wrong, but your kind of people can be quite difficult with foreigners like me. At least I am not American, am known here as South African, which is good since South Africa stays out of this crazy war today, thank God."

He looks at me and then at his feet, and digs with a stick in the sand. Then he starts, "Look, William, all our people are one big family. In a war like this we've become even closer to each other. I know the stepbrother of my uncle who owns all these goats. His name is Ebrahim. He got weapons at home, and explosives in his house, and he goes to meetings and travels a lot in the country. I would have to ask him, and he might not listen to me. He usually only laughs at me and says that I always smell like my sheep, and that I am stupid like a goat!"

Well, I can see what role my friend has to play in this family:

A shepherd, responsible for goats, sheep and more goats, and they've kept him uneducated. But Harun is clever. He pulls so much info out of his toy, and he reads and surfs the internet all day. Thanks goes to Obama for a free internet connection in the whole desert.

"Okay, can you introduce me to your uncle and family?"

"That will not be easy. You are a foreigner for them, but I will tell them about our friendship, and why you are here. I need to find the right time to get you in. It might take a few days."

"That's fine. What we've got is time. You will see the right opportunity, and introduce me."

A week later, when I get to the camp fire, he is very quiet, but then he smiles. He says he's spoken to his uncle. He told him that he'd made a great friend, who would like to farm goats back home in South Africa after his job is done. That was clever, and not even so far away from the truth, so this gets me a smile on my face too.

"So, what is the plan?"

"We will have tea together in the morning, behind the bazaar. I know where, and will take you there."

"Okay, let's do that. I need to see who we might be dealing with, and I am sure we will have more meetings, till I open up what I've got in mind. I hope you didn't mention too many details about our idea?"

"No! I will never!"

I have a bit of a sleepless night before the meeting at the bazaar. Can it be that I am talking to terrorists now? Gosh, that wasn't the idea at all. The idea was an adventurous book, maybe followed by an entertaining action movie! I really don't want to get into trouble, and particularly not here. Well, now we've started the fire…

Luckily, by now my kitchen is pretty well organized, and I don't need to spend too much time in the mornings. I've got my food supplier, and a really good bookkeeper, and I check the stock once a day. My seven different dishes can be cooked perfectly by my kitchen staff, and so I am off to meet Harun at the Bazaar. Ah, there he is. Oh man, here his goat smell is even stronger than out in the desert.

He pushes me in a hurry, urging me to follow him, which I do. We walk, nearly run, through all kind of passages, across markets, up and down stairs, through a back door, and finally reach a public tea place, crowded with people and buzzing with talk. Most either ignore me totally, or look at me like they would kill me. Lovely atmosphere. Oh, what would I give to have this meeting at our lovely V&A waterfront in Cape Town!

Harun points to an old man at a table in a corner. They mumble something in their language, and then the old man points to the other two chairs.

I try to introduce myself, and to give him my hand, but there is no reaction. He only turns his head to Harun and speaks to him. A waiter pours us hot tea.

The old man looks at me. I can see the hard years of desert life in his sunburned face. The dried out skin looks thick, like the leather of my boots. His grey eyelashes are hanging over his eyes, and the bit I can see of his face is just hard. While he enjoys his tea, he stares at me from his dark eyes and mumbles a few words to Harun between sips. After about ten minutes, Harun gets up and tells me it is time to go.

I look questioningly at him, but he just repeats, "Let's go".

I haven't even touched my hot tea, although a cold beer would be finished by now.

Okay. I get up and say bye-bye to the old man, who ignores me again. Then we disappear between the people and across alleys. But I cannot wait, and ask Harun, "What was that all about?"

He says, "Don't worry. All is fine. He read your face and eyes, that's all!"

"Oh great! And what did he read? That I was dying for a cold beer?"

"Ai, you are stupid. My uncle is a very wise old man, and he says he can see in your eyes that you get what you want, and that you are determined to get things done, the way you want!"

Well, that's how I see myself too. Clever old man, his uncle.

"But I need to talk to him!"

"You can't, he doesn't speak any English."

"What? Oh damn! And now?"

"Hey, German, you need to be patient. You always say we have time. This was first contact, and he will let me know when we need to meet again."

"So what does he know so far?"

"Now he knows that you are going to America and that you can deliver a message in an impressive way which will scare America!"

"Hmmm... okay, that's a nice way to put it. It sounds even very harmless. Is that enough for him to sign a five million dollar cheque?"

"Oh, you don't understand. Just wait. He needs to speak to people, who will speak to people, and they will speak to other people, till the right person speaks to us! That's how it works here. For now, we need to wait."

And there we are at our parking place: his stubborn old donkey, and my rusty Landy. These two are so different, like Harun and myself, but they both do their job.

I get back to the kitchen. It is nearly lunchtime and the first workers are already having tea. It smells good here; chicken curry day. I am happy with the healthy food we prepare here, even if I miss fresh salads. But we have lots of vegetables and I still feel healthy and strong, and do my daily workout, which relaxes body and mind.

Luckily, one doesn't get any reminder of women or anything erotic here. They are all dressed in black with scarves over their heads, and even my experienced eyes cannot imagine what sexy curves are below their clothing. This is just no place for flirts and dates. How I miss my Cape Town, where we have at least five women per man, and beautiful ones at that. What a paradise it is. Maybe I should become a Moslem after the successful mission, and get a harem? Why buy a book when you live in a library, as they used to say in Thailand.

The crowd of men comes and queues for food, the good smell of the huge pots getting them to smile. I am surprised by how easy this job has turned out to be.

Well, it is more the circumstances that one gets paid for, but I've nevertheless got the feeling that I am making the best out of it. At least I save ninety-five percent of my salary, since I have free living in my air-conditioned container, and free food and free transport. And no need for fancy clothing. Here I can wear my old stuff. That's the comfy way I like it. Unshaved and with my turban, I can mingle with the locals.

I always wonder myself, at how quickly I can adapt to a different world, even to the unbelievable volume of tea I drink every day, but it really keeps the mind clear, which I do need in order to make the perfect plan. I wake up at night and make notes, and think while I look into the bright stars here. The plan is still a thin skeleton, with lots of questions and twists to be answered, but it is fun. My fantasy and my adventurous imagination are my biggest tools, and this mission will be a masterpiece – or a master peace – in the end.

But if this mission is not going to change my life forever, I might end up opening a pizza place, or an alcohol free brewery, in Afghanistan!

I've had a vision about my book or movie for some time, but now that it seems that I might get to write it, that it all might become reality, that seems a huge twist – a magnificent twist, thanks to Harun and his thought. And if nobody likes the book and nobody from the movie industry shows any interest or attention? Well, then at least I would have written it out of my mind.

I am getting excited by every thought, and the fact that we might really do something crazy and impressive blows my mind. So far it blows only my mind, but we might end up blowing something much bigger and important, something the whole world will get shown and will know. Damn, this is getting fucking scary! I try to calm myself down by telling myself that I won't hurt any lives at all, even if scenario two has to come into play.

I also have to work on an escape route, after the fulfilled mission. Let's pray to God that it will all be done in a movie only, and that there will be no penalty to expect. I have to focus on this, that it all will be cleared and done well.

Now, every evening when I get to the campfire, Harun asks when we will go, and I have to calm him down, which is quite difficult. I don't want to give away any details of what I've got in mind to do, and for now I can pass the ball back to him, because I haven't heard from his people and the lovely tea meeting is already a week ago.

But he is quite sure that they will contact us again.

I am very nervous now when I walk on my own in town. Sometimes I think I am being followed, but I am only a slave of my fantasy. Nobody knows anything so far, and nobody can read my mind, where all is filed. My handwritten notes are in German and I can hardly read them myself, so the idea and plans must be safe.

I ask Harun if he can imagine leaving his world – the goats, the desert – not knowing when or if he'll come back? He says yes, of course, he wants to live, and he's got nothing to lose, only to win! Where he is right, he is right. I've always had the same thoughts. If you do not go one day, to see where you would get if you go, you will never know where you would have got, if you went!

I need to think for him too, by planning our mission. I know he will follow me, as his goats and sheep follow him.

I tell him that the longer we are here, the more money I can save and the better we can plan. And that we have to get him travel documents, and, well, maybe jeans and a shirt.

It scares me too, that I cannot look into his head. I know what is in store, because I have been where we need to go. He is just fascinated from pictures and our talks, but he might be scared out in the real world. Can he cope, I wonder?

Well, I shall see it as a back-packer trip for the first part, and that is actually the way we have to start our journey, so there is nothing to lose if we do things right, slowly and surely.

By the time I can start building up the equipment needed for our mission, we will already have been travelling for a few weeks. If then he makes problems, then we will split and everybody goes home. As for me, the whole idea was always to work here for a maximum of six months, save the cash, and go home to start another business idea anyway.

It will be Harun who will end up in the desert again.

He is so curious. "Please tell me, what we gonna do?"

It seems fair enough to give him some info, but I try to make it short.

"Well, first we need to get you out of here, and get you a passport, best a South African one, like I have."

"Where?" he shouts.

"In a very lovely city where I have contacts, but first you need to get there, and hey, we will go by airplane."

Oh, his face goes wild now, smiling from ear to ear.

"Yes," I say, "we will fly, maybe on different routes. Maybe I have to go earlier."

"No! No!" he screams. "We do all together!"

"Yes, we will, as best as we can."

"And then we fly to America?"

"No, we will go by boat to America, because we have to bring our equipment with us!"

"By boat? Over water?"

"Yes, across the Atlantic, my boy!"

"I can't swim!"

"What? Okay, that's something you will have to learn before we can leave. And we start with the first lesson tomorrow at that old water reservoir in the valley."

"That's dirty!"

"Well, then get us a blow-up pool on the market!?"

"There is a little dam high up in the mountains, let's go there."

"Okay, we will do. Tomorrow I'll come earlier in the afternoon, and bring you some shorts to wear."

"And what boat?" he asks, while he types *boat* into Google.

"A sailing boat. We will buy a catamaran, or better a trimaran, in Africa."

"Africa," he yells, and types it into Google.

"Yes, in Africa, in Mozambique." He keeps on typing. "Okay, my friend, I've given you some homework now I guess. I'm going back. I'll see you tomorrow for swimming lessons."

He can't take his eyes off his little screen, even while he waves good night.

I do understand. If my mind is cooking, then his must be boiling. "Good night my friend," I say.

This night I have to take a different route home. The one road is blocked and, as usual, nobody can or will tell me why. I don't care. I enjoy this rocky mountain pass, even it takes two hours. While I am driving I picture the sailing trip. I've only sailed once, in 1990, from Cabo Verde to Brazil. Two weeks at sea; what a wonderful experience it was.

At the time, I was kind of stuck on these Islands, and got approached by a German skipper, who'd sailed down from Spain and was looking for a deck hand when I bumped into him on a Russian ship that brought wheat and maize from North Africa to Mindelo, the biggest harbour on Cabo Verde.

The German captain bought diesel from the Russian captain, where he heard that I was going with this 275-metre ship to Brazil. He asked me if I know about sailing. When I spotted his thirteen-metre luxury yacht from deck, I had to make up some stories about my sailing experience in the Mediterranean. He took it seriously, stupid as he was. His only English was, "I am a Hamburger".

Anyway, it turned out to be a very enjoyable sailing trip; easy too. We set sail at once, and cruised with the Passat wind from Mindelo via the beautiful island of Fernando de Noronha to Recife, in Brazil.

I was on night shift from 22h00 till 06h00 in the morning, sitting behind the auto pilot and watching the sea for big ships that might come too close. I loved the nights out there, in a nutshell on the Atlantic, reading *Gilgamesh*, a book about a bible-ish hero who fights to get his father's land back.

So, that is my sailing experience and I'll have to read myself into sailing skills. Harun needs to learn swimming, and I to navigate at sea. At least I know I don't get sea sick.

The next day I bring him a pair of my shorts. The mountain pool Harun mentioned is too far away and, while we walk to the old water tank, I explain to him the theory of swimming and let him already do some exercise with his arms in the air. I make it clear to him that he has to learn it. Without swimming, it's a no go!

This filthy water tank is nearly one metre high, with brownish water; not very inviting, but it will do the job. To be fair, I climb in first, not knowing what kind of water creatures are living in it. He looks strange, in just my shorts, but seems comfortable.

He realizes that this is part of a long way now. Lucky for us, it's hot here, and the water is warm, like tea, even if it stinks. I hold him like a kid in my arms and let him do the movements, first arms only, then legs. After ten minutes I let him loose, and of course he goes down – that's part of the learning process. I tell him to keep his mouth closed, but he wants to scream and swallows water. He is upset, but I tell him once more that he has to keep on doing the moves, and we try again, and again.

He picks it up quickly, and after an hour he can keep himself on the surface.

In the next days he learns how to swim across the eight-metre tank, and seems to be enjoying it. I am glad. We will bring his swimming skills to perfection when we are in Mozambique. There we will have lots of time, and a beautiful beach, while preparing our boat.

He is proud of himself; me too. I see that he is willing to learn, and to take risks. And I understand that he will do as I say. That's very important for the whole mission. As acknowledgement of what he has achieved, I let him keep my shorts.

Back at the campfire, he shows me the pics of boats and Mozambique he's found on the internet. Well, the boat pics he found in some classy magazine, and I need to explain to him that our boat will be very, very different from these, without TV or any luxury, and definitely with no helicopter on deck. It is okay, since what does he know about luxury?

Mozambique he likes, since on more or less every beach picture he's spotted some goats at the sand.

We sit around our fire and get dry again. Now he is full of questions. He wants to know how we will build a bomb.

"A bomb?" I ask him.

"Yes, don't we need a big bomb to make the damage?"

"Yes, my friend, a kind of a bomb, more a huge grenade, or let's call it self-built missile, which we will also build there in Mozambique, on our boat, if we get the ingredients there."

"How?"

"That's a big question. I'll show you how when we are there."

"With what you build a bomb?" he wants to know.

"That's the reason we'll do it in Mozambique. Let's say we recycle a lot of old unused war-rubbish, which got left behind in Mozambique after its crazy civil war. It's going be a job to get the stuff and put it into place, but I have friends in Mozambique, since I worked in a funny backpacker place in Chimoio in 2007.

"In these month I got to know a lot of interesting people. You will see and meet them. I'm glad we will be under no time pressure – well, depending on the budget we will have available by then.

"It is already three weeks now, since we met your uncle. Can't you contact him again?"

"No, we must wait for him."

Next day I stroll over to the market and bazaar, looking for new spices and more vegetables, but my seventh sense tells me to be on guard. Just as I start to feel really uncomfortable, I am pressed against a wall. I feel a hand on my arm, and a voice in English saying, "Come with us, William." It is a young man, in jeans and t-shirt, big, black sun glasses and unshaven cheeks. He takes me by surprise. I ask him where to, and who is he? He only answers that I wanted to meet them, and that I will now.

A few old movie scenes pass through my brain. I haven't done anything wrong, so this might be the long-awaited meeting, even if it is a bit harsh. Well, I have to walk with him, through a few alleys, and then we step into a house, walking down a few corridors and up some steps.

In front of a door he says, "Don't be scared, but I have to blindfold you."

Now I look at him, a bit scared, and also realize that he is not alone anymore. Then he even says, "Please, don't be scared. It is better this way."

Well, okay, but I only wanted to write a book. They blindfold me, and now I've got one guy holding my right arm, another one keeping my left arm tight, and the door is opened and I am pushed through, and put on a chair. Silence is in the room. A new voice says, "Hallo," and he uses my full name, which not even Harun knows. "Is that you?"

He wants confirmation, and I say, "Yes, that's me, and who are you?" I get told that I don't need to know that and he reads a version of my CV to me, with details from my four-year army career in Germany, details which have never been filed, or so I'd thought. He even knows that, in addition to the four years in the German paratroops, I'd spent a few months in the foreign legion in France, where I'd also got special education in explosives.
"So you know about explosives?"
"Yes, I do."
"And where will you get your explosives?"
"In Africa," I answered.
"Where and what from?" he asks, a bit louder now.

I take a deep breath, and get nervous, since I really don't know who is asking me. I don't want to get locked up somewhere for having the idea of writing a book about a sabotage in the United States.

He repeats his question again, and adds that he wants and needs to know.

I answer, a bit cheekily, that I will get it in a country where a war is over, and the stuff stayed behind. Bang! I get hit on my head. It seems that this answer doesn't make him happy.

And his reaction doesn't make me happy.

But then he apologizes and says that he didn't hit me, it was the youngster close to me. He talks again. He says he has been told that I might be able to do something for them, and that they appreciate any help, so I should share what my plan is.

"Yes, I understand that, and, yes, I asked to meet you guys, but I really want to see who I am talking to, because this is not a game and I am even scared to share details with Harun." It is silent for a minute, and then I hear steps, men leaving the room, and a door is closed again.

He rips off my blindfold. I really hadn't expected any face other than one like his, with black beard, black sunglasses and a turban. He reaches out his hand, and introduces himself as Achmeth. Hmmm, sure, one of the Achmeths.

I am given tea, and see that I am in a well-furnished, clean lounge. There is even a laptop and a webcam.

"Hey, do you copy what's going on up here, our whole conversation?" He only smiles.

I try to win some time by sipping the hot tea slowly.

And inside me is only the wish to get out of here. Seeing that he is quite comfy, I get up and walk towards him, away from his webcam, and I don't want to say any more words about what my plan is here. I ask him if I can use his laptop, and he moves it over to me.

I go on Google and type something in. A picture comes up and I turn the screen to him and explain, with a clear hand sign, that this is the target which I've got in mind.

He stares, speechless, at the screen. He has the same look that Harun has had for the past two months. He even takes his sunglasses off and looks in my eyes, which gives me a look into his shaded, sixty-something, yellowish, brown eyes.

"You are sure you can do that?" he asks. I just nod very convincingly with my head.

Now, he screams a name, the door opens, men come in, keep me tight and blindfold me again. Surprised, I get scared and scream and ask, "What now?"

There is no answer, no word from them. They push me through the corridors, down the stairs and into a car. The car drives off and my whole life passes by. I listen to every noise, but, before I can get even more scared, the car stops, and they push me out.

I lie in the dust, but I am alive, no damage at all, just my heart pumping out of my throat. I am outside the city wall, in a quiet area, but I know where I am. I get up and walk to my Landy, drive straight to my container, and grab the hidden whiskey and a cigarette. Did I just have a meeting, or an interview, with terrorists? Or was it a joke?

It can't be a joke. They knew details about me, things I don't even have written proof of. I don't like that, not at all. And what conversation was it? Well, damn sure this was not the CIA. Nevertheless, I am still shivering all over. They know everything about me, and I don't even know who I spoke to.

I finish another double whisky and get back in my car, and drive out to Harun. He is surprised to see me that early, and he sees immediately that I am different and totally excited.

"What happened," he asks?

I sit down, staring down at the fire, and say to him, "You won't believe it. I will tell you all, just let me calm down first." I look into the fire and recall what happened. Gosh, this is serious, and now I've really got cold feet, even in the desert heat, and at a fire.

"Tell me what happened?" Harun shouts.

"They took me in for a talk!"

"Who?"

"I don't really know, but these must be men that your uncle knows."

"That is good," Harun says. "Tell me what they said."

"Well, they caught me on the bazaar, took me to a house, blindfolded and questioned me. The scary thing was that they know everything about me, even lots of things I didn't tell you, and things I didn't know were filed anywhere."

"So what else? What did you tell them?"

"They wanted to know where I would get the explosives from, and I really didn't feel like sharing that with them, not knowing who they are."

"But that is good. At least they came to you, so they must be interested."

"They should be interested, but I wonder if they take us seriously, and think we're capable of what I'm planning. This was a very interesting meeting. I felt already like I'm in a movie, and was actually impressed when they left me alone with the main talker."

"They did? Who was it?"

"I don't know. He introduced himself as Achmeth, but how many Achmeths are here? That's like Michael in Germany. And they all look the same to me, with their black beards."

"Okay, but you don't have to be scared. That is how they are, and they might be more scared than you!"

"I am happy that they showed an interest. I think that is a step forward. And I got a strong feeling that they will come back to us."

"Why?"

"Well, I showed him the target, and then he got nearly speechless and kicked me out, and they dropped me outside the city wall. I was just happy that nothing happened to me. But now, when I think it through and over, that's the contact we needed. Now we have just to wait again. Now we've started a fire, now there are people out there who might believe we can and will do what we promised."

I still can't believe I am dealing with terrorists. Oh my God, am I now a terrorist myself? It has gone beyond stupid adventure boy talk.

"Tell me, what target did you show? What target will it be anyway?"

"My dear friend Harun, please don't ask that. I believe it is better and safer for you to know as little as possible, till we get really started. I promise you, I'll keep you updated as necessary. But now I really want to get started as soon as possible. I want to get out of here. I want to Walk the Talk! Next week it is my third pay-day."

He looks excitedly at me and I say, "What? Do you think we will go soon? We should. I can write the book for the movie while we travel. As I said the other day, I already feel like I'm in a movie, so let's get it done."

He comes and puts his arm around me, and looks into my eyes. "Listen William, I know you are worried about me, and yes, I do know it is something big we will do, and I will give my life for it. Well, I will get a real life for it!

Here I am like a two-legged goat, nothing else, and I tell you, William, if you don't go, then I go alone!"

That makes me laugh. He understands it right, he read my thoughts, and yes, I should stop worrying too much about him. He is a strong Moslem, and he will survive, however it comes. We take a chance, and life happens when you make new plans.

I get to the kitchen too late for lunch, but it all seems fine. They wonder where I've been. It is the first time I've been late, but I thank them all; they managed without me. I am wondering if I should tell my head chef that I might have to leave suddenly, but that it will go on here. I've trained him in all departments. He is Indian and speaks good English, so if I disappear, he can take over. I will resign by email, shortly before I leave.

I can't believe that three months here are nearly over, and what's been developing during that time. What's going to happen will be something nobody's ever done or tried before.

There are still plenty of gaps in my plan that I have to sort out, but it will happen while we are out there and doing it. So far, I know where to go, and what to do, and yes, I smile when I play it through. It's too funny. We're going to do something, the details of which I'll keep in a book, in the hope that a movie gets made accordingly. If I could speed up time, where will we be one year from now? It's all open; lots can happen. But whatever happens, I will have a beef steak with cold beer in Bangkok, and I will have some quality fun. I won't visit my brother, who lives on Phuket, because he would ask what I am doing, and I would tell him. I prefer to tell people what I have done, not what I am going to do. I wish politicians and presidents would do the same.

For a change, I have an afternoon sleep in my container. What happened today will change my life, and I don't care. I am happy it happened, even if nothing got sorted, but I feel that something has started!

I fall asleep for two hours, then have a strong coffee, check that all is prepared for supper in the kitchen, and out to Harun.

These days he is just happy and smiling, wearing proudly only a bright yellow, western world shorts.

"Oh my friend, I will get you dressed in Thailand, and I will introduce you to the world. We're gonna miss our evenings here, but better evenings will come. Oh yes, evenings with more fun involved and the pleasure of knowing we are on our way."

He always gets a supper box from me. He loves the food and he'd better get used to my cooking. He will visit his uncle tomorrow morning, and ask for the Afghan passport they made for him when he wanted to join their army. I told him to ask who the men were that spoke to me. I am dying to know what they think of us, and what comes next.

I ask him if he will tell his family when he goes. He shakes his head. No, he can't, and he can't lie, but he will leave a letter, and tell them he'll be back in a year. Well, let's hope so. Then he asks me all these questions about Bangkok, and Africa; too many questions, but I understand. The info about Bangkok must be mind-blowing for him, just as my Thailand experience two years ago was for me. When I thought I had experienced all this world has to offer, Thailand was, even for me, another eye-opener. I need to watch him, and when we're there, take care of him. We might have to hang around for up to a week in Bangkok. I know the cheapest flights from there are with Kenyan airways, Jambo Africa. By then, he will have a new foreign passport, like I've got. Let me think which name I shall give him in it. Hmmm, I will let him decide. I'm sure he will come up with a name he likes.

Gosh, now we even have Thai music out of his iPad; nice memories for me.

Shall I blame IT now, for what we're doing? Isn't it amazing, how this technical equipment can change our lives? I remember when I went to Mozambique for the first time, in 1997 for a visa break. Most of the houses, bridges and walls had been painted red, Coca Cola-designed the year Coca Cola had built a huge plant there.

When I went to Mozambique in 2007, all was mostly painted yellow, and designed by MTN, the South African cell phone service provider. I travelled as usual on public transport, and nearly every Mozambiquan had a cell phone – even those without shoes or shirts had a cell phone stuck to their hand – and street children didn't sell cashew nuts and coconuts anymore; no, they sold damn airtime for cell phone users!

For the cost of the calls made, when the locals called home to say they couldn't find cheap food and mama should put the kids to bed, they might have got food next day. Yes, with what this call costs they could have fed the kids. The third world does not need cell phones, hallo, but the companies are so unscrupulous as to take even the money of the poorest for useless communication services.

The time I worked – well I actually cooked there too, in a backpacker in Chimoio north west Mozambique, close to Mutare on the Zimbabwe border – I met a lot of these funny volunteers and development helpers, who came mostly from Europe. They'd been very well educated in their home country, and were now nicely paid in Euros while living in the third world.

They came as optimists to make all better, but became shortly after arrival realists, realizing that everything there is a fuck up, with no rules or laws, but endless corruption, and after two months or so they became tourists, playing golf for two Euro in neighbouring Zimbabwe, and having wild parties every day.

I experienced the corrupt life. I went with an Austrian guy to a village, a hundred k's north. There he approached the local chief, and told him it was his lucky day, that he would drill him a borehole and fix a water pump for him, free of any costs, as help from his little hometown community in Austria. The chief looked at the big truck with drill equipment, and Heinz explained to him the water pump that would be installed in the middle of his village. Then the chief turns around, and asks what he gets if he is allowed to set up the pump? Hmmmm, what kind of question is that?

Well, he wanted a Toyota 4x4, a hundred thousand dollars in cash, and at least one credit card! Oh, is that all? "Listen old man, I will make sure that your people have got water available 24/7 in their village, that woman and children don't have to walk twenty kilometres and nine hours a day, to carry their daily water supply on their heads!"

Yes, the chief said, he understands. But, what will they do otherwise all day?

Well, there's no answer for that. Nobody was prepared for such thinking. The chief shook hands, and repeated, "Get me a new nice Toyota 4x4, and we'll talk again. Yes, thank you."

That is Africa!

But these are stories Harun cannot understand, and he doesn't have to.

He will enjoy Mozambique, that I know. There's plenty of music and girls, sunshine and goats! Bangkok will kill his brain in a storm, with the hectic pace, the climate, the concrete, and its flair and nightlife, not to forget its girls.

He studied this chapter online, and knows what I am talking about, but for him it just sounds too good to be true, and unbelievable, so, for this moment and time, I just confirm this: "It's all marketing, it's not as it says in all these promotion and ads you see."

He is counting the hours as I do. In three days it is pay-day, and we might be off, although we still need to hear from his people. But again, it all comes differently than expected.

One day, after lunch, I see a high number of military police and tanks driving around town, much more than I have ever seen all at once before. Something must be going on, but nobody can tell me what's happened. When I get stopped for a routine control of my papers, by a multinational unit that includes a German soldier, I hear what occurred. A whole convoy of supply trucks for the army, coming from Pakistan, got hijacked; trucks with fuel, ammunition and equipment, a total of fifty-five trucks which need to be stopped and reprocessed. I am glad I am not a soldier here. It smells like big trouble.

This afternoon, no vehicle is allowed to leave the city. I am stuck, and Harun will not know where I am. I've never thought to supply him with an email address, stupid me. We get approached to stay in our houses, and are told not to walk on the streets or outside the city. What is that now supposed to mean?

Then, at nearly sunset time, we hear the fighter planes passing over town, a high number at full speed. Minutes later, I hear machine gun fire, grenades and missiles, a loud firework, maybe not even ten miles away. The planes fly up and down a few times, and repeat their attack, most probably to save the hijacked convoy. The whole fight lasts not even half an hour, and then it is silence again in the sky. I jump in my Landy and want to drive out and see, because it all must have been close to Harun's camp. I hope he is safe. But there is no way or chance for me to leave the city. They don't even check papers, they just block any access road and send me back. I even try various different ways, where I know some of the soldiers, but it seems hopeless. I am stuck in the city. A second try, close to midnight, doesn't work either.

So, I sit alone in my container, my last bottle whiskey nearly finished – another sign that it might be time to go.

Next morning I get up early, shortly before sunrise, jump again into my Landy and drive out of the city. Now there is only routine control of my papers, and off I go. Already, after a few miles, I smell burned stuff, and see a few burned-out, rolled-over trucks burning on the drive way. When I turn off to the camp I can't believe my eyes, but have to believe my nose. This scene reminded me of a old western movie, where new settlers shot the buffalos from a train. Here I see an endless number of dead goats and sheep, some still burning, some just smelling like burned meat and animal skin. Oh, it just stinks. I speed up, and then I spot Harun in the yellow shorts, kneeing down by a dead goat. I stop the car and walk towards him. He is in tears, and his face is black from smoke and ashes.

"German, where you been?" he shouts.

"I am sorry, my friend. I tried to come, but they wouldn't let anyone leave the city! What happened? Please tell me."

"Nearly at sunset, planes came, flying very low. First they were shooting at trucks, far away at the old road, over the pass. Then they came back and shot only fire bombs down. The goats went mad, running away everywhere, but it was so loud, and the animals didn't know where to run to, and they got hit by the fire and went off in flames, running even faster while they were burning, till they broke down and burned brutally to death. They were screaming till death set in. It was horrible. I tried to chase as many as possible into the little cave, but alone I couldn't save them from the craziness."

I looked around. The scenery that was offered to me was horrible; hundreds of burned goats and sheep all over the valley. Only far at the back, I saw a few alive.

I hug him, and say what I think, that this is a further sign from the universe that we have to go, now, as soon as possible, tomorrow is pay-day! And we walk towards my Landy.

Oh shit, even his good donkey is lying there dead. Harun sinks down on his knees and hugs the dead body of his other best friend. Oh no, what a fuck up. Sure, one could apply for compensation, but it will take ages. Let his uncle do that.

So now, his "enemy", America, has made a massacre of his animals, which will be totally ignored by the authorities and the press. Do these pilots think the whole world is a Playstation? Damn idiots!

Harun looks up into the sky, he lifts up his hand and screams:
"YOU SHOT MY SHEEP, MR PRESIDENT!"

I can feel his anger, and see the tears running down his ash-stained face. He is not going to take that shit, he will seek justice!

Enough is enough. I am as terribly pissed off as he is now. I don't mind anymore showing America, what is NOT a Playstation.

Now they are really asking me to do what we have planned. Someone has to do it! And we will, because we can!

We won't make a massacre with blood there in America, but their authorities, the media and the whole world will be a witness. And they won't be able to ignore us, not at all, that I do know!

"Come. Come with me in the car. We'll drive to your uncle and get your passport. It is high time that we get out of here. We were just lucky. We could have been killed while sitting around our campfire too!"

I put my arm around him and walk with him to the Landy. He is in shock. Well, he could have got hit as well, he was just very lucky.

First we need to go to town. I have to check my kitchen and workers. He doesn't mind. He gets in the car with his few belongings, and doesn't look back. His tears are still running down his cheeks.

I drop him at my container, where he can wash himself, and I give him jeans and a shirt. Then I check on lunch, and there is a letter with a cash up slip. My monthly salary is already paid in. That's good to know. What a relief, because I've really had enough of this warzone shit.

While I walk back to the container, a man approaches me. He wears sunglasses, turban, beard, the usual, but he speaks a proper accent-free English. Oh, damn, it's Achmeth. He asks if we can talk, and he is alone, so I say, "Yes, let's talk, what about?"

"We want you to do what you promised, do it for us, and, yes, we will pay you a high reward, you will see, but only when it's done. You have my word and Allah's word. You will get paid highly if that job is done." Then he doesn't let me talk, but walks off, leaving me once again speechless.

I run to my container to tell Harun what happened. He's actually watched the conversation from far, and runs towards me, sporty in jeans; a new boy!

"What happened," he asks.

I tell him about the conversation, and that we've been promised to be paid, but only after a successful mission, and how much nobody mentioned, and, oh yes, I nearly forgot, Achmeth gave me a piece of paper with two email addresses, one for me, including a password for access, that they'll use to contact us, and the other to be used to contact Achmeth. I am to use them only shortly before, or after, the sabotage and to use only a few words always, not naming people, places or times.

TIME TO GO

"Okay, I got paid, I am ready to go. Let's go to your uncle."

So we drive to his uncle's little home outside the city on the other side of the mountains. His uncle is sitting in front of the house, as if expecting Harun. He hugs him for a short second, and tells him he knows what has happened. Then he gives Harun his passport, which he has already to hand, as if he already knew that Harun would go.

He's heard from his comrades that we will do something big, which might even call off the war, and that if so, we will get paid a lot of money, as soon as the results are proved.

"So you will be rich, my son, and you will start a family, and have a home. Come back when the job is done. Forget about the goats and sheep. They will breed and breed and multiply again, and live under our sun from the little bit of dry grass, as we will live on this land from what Allah gives us. Nothing and nobody will ever stop us, and if you can make life peaceful for us again, then off you go, go with Allah, and make us proud." Having said this, he gives Harun an old, dirty cotton bag, and he says that he is sorry, he's never paid Harun all these years for guarding his goats, but there was also no need; what does he need money for out in the desert?

"Take my savings, and use them wisely." The bag is packed full with dollar notes, small dirty notes, but lots of them. Then he hugs Harun again, turns around and walks into his house. Harun seems happy and relieved. I guess he must feel like I did when I left the German army after four years, and got a twenty thousand Mark package.

Later in the evening we count nearly ten thousand dollars in cash, all in relatively small notes, old and dirty. This must be the savings of his uncle from the last twenty years. Together with my fifteen thousand Euro, and the hopefully loaded credit cards, this money makes a difference. We can get lots done, and now we can really go, yes we can!

Since there is hardly any civil air traffic from Afghanistan out of the country, and what there is is extremely expensive, and we've both only got a few things and one bag each, we decide on the overland bus to Pakistan, into the capital Karachi. From there we will get a flight to Bangkok, since they've got regular air traffic, and we will save quite some money. We have to budget extremely carefully, but hopefully the next "income" will last forever.

We sit together in the bazaar, drinking tea, both very quiet. I am making notes, what and how to do. He's found out about the bus to Karachi. It will be a torturous drive. Every time I do such an overland bus trip, I swear afterwards that this one will be the last one, but it's so cheap, and the bus leaves today.

In 1998 I took the bus from Jo'burg to Blantyre in Malawi, all the way up through Mozambique. I'd asked how long it would take, and they'd said between fifty and ninety hours. We were quick; it took only eighty hours, but what a nightmare of a ride.

So Harun organized the bus for us, and got information that I can get into Pakistan with my German passport, and get a visa at the border. He doesn't need a visa with an Afghanistan passport. I am so looking forward to the landing in Bangkok, its restaurants and its nightlife; I'm going back to life. And then, from there our mission will finally start, bringing a vision to reality.

He looks at me and speaks up. "William, please never ever ask me again if I am ready and if I really want to go. I am ready since we spoke about the idea, and now look how far we are! This is our last day here, and we've got quite some money."

Will it be enough? It has to be. There is no further cash to wait for, except for the credit cards which we will check first thing after landing. Then we will budget and take it easy.

"I wonder what they will pay us if the target goes hop?" I ponder.

"They know what you will ask from the movie industry, I told them, And they will pay accordingly. That's what my uncle told me."

This sounds promising and impressive and I still hope deep inside me that we won't have to do it! I will ask for confirmation by email, once we are there and ready. And I don't actually see it as a payment from the Taliban. Instead, I see it as a fee for delivering a strong message; that sounds much better to me.

Then we walk to my container. I pack what I need, but leave lots of old clothes behind, and outside on the washing line, so nobody will think I've left for good. In Thailand we'll both get some cheap shorts and shirts, all that we need for the next few months. It's time that Harun gets a human, modern outfit.

I will only email my resignation from Bangkok. I really don't want to get stuck here, arguing with management. The kitchen will go on, no doubt about it. Now we've got a more important job to do!

It's time to walk to the bus. It is crowded already, that old MAN chassis absolutely overloaded, like in Africa, with goats and chickens on the roof carrier, and bags piled two metres high. Harun does the talk and the tickets, and then we sneak in and get two front seats next to each other. We keep our little bags on our laps. I wear my old leather boots, each filled with nearly five thousand US in cash. It's safer that way.

The credit cards I keep inside the chassis of my laptop. They also shouldn't be found on us at any checkpoint.

An hour too late, and crowded with passengers standing in the aisle of the bus, the diesel stinker starts moving. We laugh at each other and clap hands: high five! But then, not even three kilometres into our journey, the first UN checkpoint comes, and we're all out of the bus, undergoing body and passport checks. The one soldier remembered me.

"Hi William, where are you off to?"

"Believe it or not, even I need a break after three months. I don't get flown out every two month on government expense like you guys. I want to hike a few days up in the mountains bordering Pakistan."

He laughs, claps my shoulder and says, "Take care, and see you later."

The whole procedure takes nearly one and a half hours. Every bag is checked for weapons or anything dodgy, and for some passengers the journey is already over, most probably because of missing identity documents.

I lean back, and enjoy the scenery. A beer would be nice, but not available. I fall asleep on Harun's shoulder, and his head leans against the window. The solid excitement in us does need a deserved rest, and there is nothing to do other than to dream of the time to come.

We wake up in a little village. People sell tea and some baked stuff. Harun supplies us with something eatable, and the drive continues after ten minutes.

It is all dirt roads. The men that I fed have to tar it all. I hope that someone else will feed them as well in future. My job here is done, and I believe well done, and with this thought I smile and I fall asleep again. The bus stops every hour for a toilet break. Even though there is no toilet around, the driver still has to stop. We go through another two checkpoints that check only the number of people, counting the heads. They seem well informed from the first check point.

Early in the morning we reach the Pakistan border. Gosh, what a shitty dirt hole. There are funny creatures hanging around, observing each person and anything else leaving this bus. Food and tea sellers approach us; even a fancy taxi driver. But we only want to get in the next bus on the other side of the border, which, looking at this endless long single queue of people trying to pass the border post and immigration, seems far away.

I feel comfy with my little backpack, not like in previous years in Africa, when all my possessions packed in my old army sack sometimes weighed up to fifty kilo's, which made it impossible to defend myself, or to run after someone when something got stolen. Here I feel like a weekend holidaymaker, even if it's going to be something totally different.

We finally reach the desk. The officers are wearing old worn out uniforms, with holes all over. They have a long chat with Harun in front of me. Then I get only a serious look, and a stamp in my passport. I love it. I'd expected to be questioned, and to be begged for a little bribe. Maybe one day, when I am really bored, I'll write a book about border posts in the whole world, and how much nerve and sweat they have cost me in the last twenty years. The guy in Boa Vista, Brazil, only gave me a visa for Venezuela because we had the same name, and at my regular border visits to renew my tourist visa during the first four years in South Africa, I was always spiked with a story, and had to fiddle my way through.

So, now we are in Pakistan.

"Hey," I clap his shoulders, "you are in a foreign country! How does that feel?"

Well, he seems disappointed, which I can understand. It seems to be still the same desert, and it actually looks like it could be around the corner from our beloved campfire.

Now there are plenty of buses waiting. I let Harun do the inquiries. It is nice to not travel alone for a change, and so far he is doing well, only complaining that he doesn't want to sit anymore, that his bum hurts. Well, tell me about it. There is hardly any foam left in these seats. I promise him a Thai massage as soon we are in Bangkok, and that verbal promise immediately takes his pain away. It seems he has read about Thai massages, clever chappie!

Ten minutes later we sit in the next bus, close to the driver, in what must be first class. The radio is doodling Arab music – every song sounds the same – and there is a funny perfume dispenser in the bus; disgusting, as I know it from Turkey, which I travelled in my childhood, Slowly the scenery starts changing, it is getting greener. Lovely! I've missed some green. Harun loves it too.

"Look, as I promised you, your life is becoming more colourful."

"Hahahah."

I can see he is happy. He's started a new life and I am his shepherd now.

Of course, my mind doesn't stop spinning while sitting in the bus.

Too many Whats? Ifs? Hows? are permanently crossing my mind. What if all fails? I might get an odd job again. And what about him?

I feel like I've adopted him.

"Stop it!" he shouts. Gosshh, can he read my mind? "Stop worrying, it all will be fine. We go with Allah, and we doing something good. You can worry when things go wrong, not now. For now, enjoy the ride, German!"

Waaoouuww, that was good. This is the kick that I need, because I always worry too much, so much that there are many things I've never tried, too worried that I would fail. How often have I been stupid? And here there are three chances still to get money in, and whatever happens, it will all end with an adventure book, which I will write as we go. Or perhaps it really becomes a movie; then we are sorted… or… yes, we become paid terrorists, spend maybe the rest of our lives on the run… or even unpaid terrorists… hmmmm..

"STOP it!" he shouts. Damn it, he reads me like a book.

Okay, time to get into a country where beer and whiskey are available; tea doesn't calm me down anymore.

Now the bus rolls on tarred road, although I don't know which is better. Dirt road is permanently bad, and one gets used to it, but a tar road, with all the hidden deep potholes, is very dangerous and uncomfortable. It gets greener and greener, and more western cars are passing by, even pretty new ones. There are also shops with more advertising and promotion. Yes, we're getting close to the capital. Once there, it is straight to the airport. I live in the hope of getting a flight immediately, and keep some dollars handy for a taxi.

"Harun, my friend, are you aware that you will fly very soon, for the first time in your life?"

He just smiles. I believe that if I were to shoot him to the moon with a rocket built by me, he would just do it. Anything is better than sitting alone in a desert.

There is the first street sign, Karachi 289 km. Okay, that can be easily another three to four hours, but by now it is pretty entertaining. There is lots to see; fancy building styles here, and the first elephants on the road. But I fall from one nap into another. That is how it happens on these long bus rides. Harun wakes me up as we enter the first suburbs of Karachi. What chaos and dirt. Oh, how I hate big, crowded cities. Harun found out that the bus stops close to the airport, which is across the road. We might not even need a taxi; sounds cool.

And here we are, Welcome to Karachi. What a mess, but already much better than any city in Afghanistan. I didn't expect too much from here, but it looks safe and organized, with lots of police around, and lots of western-style-dressed people. Okay, we're getting closer to the world.

I can't see any sign to the airport, but there are lots of taxis; let's try. I speak to one driver, saying only airport and holding a five dollar note up, which he nicks, and we are in.

I prefer it this way, instead of running around for another hour to find directions, and now we stop already. That was only a five-minute ride, just out of the chaos.

Harun gets a shock when we enter the airport building.

"It is cold here," he says, "very cold."

"Oh yes, that's an air-conditioner. They cool the air down, to make it more comfortable. You will get used to that in Bangkok, because without aircon you wouldn't be able to sleep."

I am looking for a travel agent. We will get tickets to Bangkok, and a connection flight ten days later to Nairobi in Kenya – I remember that these were the cheapest air fares to Africa – and, to get our Thailand tourist visa, we will have to show a return ticket at Bangkok airport immigration.

His head is turning 360 degrees; he's never experienced such a high-tech environment, nor seen so many relatively well-dressed people. I grab his arm and pull him to the travel agency at the end of the hall. Inside it's quiet, but also busy. It seems pretty organized and established, and I hope they can get us what we need.

Harun cannot take his eyes of the gorgeous assistant. Well, me neither, but where we are going next we will get a treat. Luckily she speaks English, as it should be at an airport like that. Okay, I tell her, we need two tickets to Bangkok for the next possible flight, and from there tickets to Nairobi in Kenya, for about ten days later.

Big as they already are, she makes big eyes and starts typing in her computer. I hope that we can get the passport for Harun in ten days time. In-between we can work on the plan of action, and yes, have some damn well-deserved holiday and a party after our desert and campfire time, I need some fun, and it seems only fair enough for him too, after over twenty years of shepherding in the hot, sandy desert.

She's got the first info: a flight to Bangkok in eight hours time, US$295. – for each of us. Nothing cheaper? No. Okay, we take that one, and the Kenyan flight goes daily, so we can change the date of departure for an extra fee. That's another US$513 each – it's all adding up, but there is no other way around. It's always painful for me to spend so much money. I cannot wait to check the credit cards, and hope that they will give us another financial push. Half an hour later we sit in a coffee place; tea for him, and a good coffee for me. We just cannot stop smiling at each other.

He says, "Thank you, William. Thank you for doing all that, and letting me be part of it, I will never regret, whatever happens." High five! There won't be any regrets. I know what is coming, although he can only fantasize so far.

We kill the waiting time, me by doing some calculations and plans, he happily back on the internet or, judging from the size of his eyes, he is already in Bangkok.

Check-in time is easy for us, with only hand luggage. Fasten seat belts, and there we take off. He is fascinated; the speed, the noise, and then the silence high up in the air, flying into a different world, beautiful. And since this is a Thai-airways flight, there is beer and all kinds of goodies available. I order two Chang Beer, but he says he doesn't want one. I tell him that I didn't ask what he wants, and remind him that he told me that he would do as I say. Cheers, and down it goes. After the first sip he checks on his taste buds, but then he smiles and orders another two beers! Yeeaaahhh, that's my man and partner in crime. Now nothing can go wrong anymore, so, after a few more beers, we snooze peacefully again.

It is only a four and a half hour flight, and before we wake up, the plane is beginning to descend; we're barely awake as we hear the noise of the brakes and the reverse power from the engines.

BANGKOK

"Welcome to Thailand, the land of smile!"

Oh... he doesn't really smile. What's up? He holds his head. Oh, how many beers did he have? Six Chang beers?

"Okay, get used to it. I'll get you a coke outside, and it will get better."

Now we cue at immigration. The friendly personnel do a proper job, and we can pass. Yeeeaahhhhh, there we go. And here are the first cash machines. I've been waiting for this moment. I put in the Visa card first, press in the pin and chose twenty thousand Baht Thai currency, which is about five hundred Euro. I wait, and then it goes tschatschtschah, and the machine gives me twenty one-thousand Baht notes. Lovely.

I do the same with the Diner's too. Only the Amex doesn't get accepted. Oh, well, we will find another way, but at least this first transaction has nearly paid back our flight tickets.

I remember a lovely hotel in downtown, not too big, but safe and clean and central, with a lovely pool area. I stop a taxi, and off we go, right into the pumping nightlife. Harun does not know where to look first. Well, at this stage and time, neither do I.

Harun sees for the first time life, and night life, which he has only observed for too long on his iPad, and there it is in reality – one can touch it, smell it hear it... and have it!

Here is our hotel, a twin room will do, and we get a nice one with a view over the pool. I sit down on my bed and take a deep breath.

"Harun, my friend, this is already a big step. We've got out of Afghanistan, got tickets, got more cash here... got a lovely place to stay... I think we should go and celebrate a bit, or do you want to sleep?"

"No! No! I will never sleep again!" he shouts. I thought so.

It is around midnight. We don't waste time on a shower, since it's still hot and very humid. Even doing nothing, one sweats here all the time. I've never liked the climate here, but otherwise, it is quite liveable.

Okay, I feel like a steak or an Eisbein. We catch a tuk-tuk taxi and I ask the driver to take us to the German Beer Garden. It's quite a drive, but that's what we will both enjoy. I make a short stop at a little shop and get two cell phones and SIM cards at a Seven-Eleven.

This is a must-have now, for him and me. If he gets lost here it would be a problem, and we need to be available and in touch with each other, whatever we do.

Here is our beer garden, home from home. We get a nice table in the corner; that's how I love it, to have the overview. I order two Bavarian draught beers for us – another thing for him to get to know – and two Eisbein, pork or not. I discussed this issue with him a long time ago, at our campfire. Then I show him the cell phone and explain how it works. He picks it all up quickly, since he is master on his iPad by now, and we call each other to check, send a few SMSs to each other, and he even takes the first pictures. It is like Christmas for him.

While I put all my Bangkok contact numbers into the new phone, he observes the place, and can't stop kicking my leg.

"Hey, William look there!" These two ladies are staring and smiling at us. Oh, they are soooo beautiful. I have a quick look, and keep on programming my cell phone

"William, look, look!"

"No, Harun, forget those two. They use the same toilet as we do!"

"What you mean?"

"Well, believe it or not, these are men!"

Now he gets cross with me. "William, this is not fair, don't do that with me!"

"Exactly, my friend, I don't do that to you. Any other man would have sent even his best friend into the knife, and would have sent him to the hotel room to make a unique, special Thai experience. These are transvestites. They were men, and have most probably some leftovers from being born as men. They've got silicon boobs and shaved legs and so on... long story... just Google it, and if you still don't believe, it will cost me a smile to prove it all to you. But I thought I'd introduce you first to real woman, isn't that better?"

He can't believe it, but he admits he has to trust me. He'd better do.

Well, I've equipped him well. He's got some cash on him, a cell phone, and the business card of our hotel, in case we split up for any reason and need to get home separately.

The Eisbein arrives, and that's even better than Christmas. All his senses must be upside down as we dig into the food. What a feast, and in future it will always be like this.

As good as the food is, his concentration is somewhere else. This is understandable; this place is known for foreigners, and the ladies of the entertainment business know that as well, and they also know exactly what they want: a rich man who will let them squeeze his purse to the limit. Their dream is to marry a rich European, so we are not the right victims today. We didn't even shower after the bus ride and flight, and we look like gypsies. We are going to change that tomorrow, although most of them wouldn't mind how we look. They see the European man in me, and they think that we must all be rich. How else could we be here just on holiday? Fair enough thoughts!

"What will we do after food?"

"We will take it easy, and stroll a bit down the road, and get some proper clothes for us, and bits and pieces of what we need, because from tomorrow I will have to make arrangements for your passport, and do some studying for boats and sailing at the pool, and then from tomorrow afternoon, it is party time."

Thanks to the one kilogram Eisbein which we each swallowed, he feels lazy too, and of course he wouldn't know how to get it all started here with the girls. Which is actually not necessary here. These girls know how to treat a virgin and an eighty-year-old pensioner; they are professionals, so I will protect him as best I can.

He is holding his tummy, so I introduce him to Jaegermeister too, that's what the doctor recommends. No... no it's not alcohol, it is medicine for full stomachs, just trust me my friend, hahahah. The after taste is even better, as the American Express card pays it all nicely.

We walk down the busy road. Damn yes, these massage salons are tempting, and the girls are just too cute, and so many, and so friendly... but no, not today. We stink and are filthy and tired. So I apologize to the girls – tomorrow... tomorrow... – till the one says, "No problem, we bath and shave you, cheap-cheap, come-come," and what a gorgeous girl she is, like the other one, like all of them, they can demolish any man's discipline... and schwup, we are inside, both of us guided by two beautiful girls, one on each arm. It is like being guided by beautiful angels, and I can't resist this temptation.

Harun looks as if he has already smoked marijuana. He is flying. Now it's all going to happen, and I won't stop it from happening. I kick his ass to wake him up and shout, "See you later at the hotel. He just nods and is guided to a huge Jacuzzi. I get taken to another one... life is beautiful.

Yes, this is what we deserve now, each of us with two sexy young girls, naked in the Jacuzzi, being spoiled rotten, beyond any man's imagination, in the land of smile.

We both spend the whole night there and enjoy what the universe serves us. Damn good it was, and damn time too, to bring my body back to life. Lovely.

We only catch up over our phones late in the morning. He can't stop talking. This boy is now a man. He could write his first book now, that I know, a book with the same title as Richard Branson's first book.

While we walk out there, he tries to tell me all the details of what happened to him, as if I wouldn't know. He is high on life's spirit, and as happy as it gets.

"We must go there again! Oh, I want to live here!"

"Oh, that's what my younger brother said six years ago, after he won a holiday to Phuket, the cosy island in the south, where he's lived happily for six years."

"Oh, you German!" he shouts, "you lived here nearly two years too! Why did you leave?"

"Why? Because of the same old problem: damn, fucking money. Like everywhere that it's nice to live, you want to grow, have a car and a house with your own Jacuzzi, and my little salary couldn't fix that, so I went back to South Africa to follow up my business dreams."

We do our shopping: two pairs of jeans each, and proper backpacks, a few shirts and shorts, underwear, sport shoes and slippers. Also some stationary for my planning activities, all paid for by Diner's Club. Lovely.

Back at the hotel, Harun discovers cable TV – the fashion channel and music channels – and watches from his double bed like a prince who just has been crowned.

I call up some contacts and make two appointments for this afternoon. It is fair to have some fun, but there are also jobs to be done. While he is stuck at the TV, I visit some other cash machines and draw a few thousand dollars in cash. So far it works, and I will push it to the limit. The banks' computer are not stupid, and might stop the cards soon, once they realize that a dead customer is withdrawing money all over Bangkok.

When I get back to the hotel, I cannot believe my eyes. There is my young prince, and who else? The two angels from last night, one on the left, one to the right. Damn he learns quickly. He makes me smile. I will leave him alone for the day; just tell him to stick to the daily budget, and that I am off to my meetings, and we will catch up for dinner. Luckily we've already made his passport pictures in a shop at the airport yesterday.

So I meet a crazy German I met two years ago in a bar in Phuket. He is now the president of a well-known motorbike club, and owns a few bars himself. He made me promise that when I was back in Bangkok I would visit and even stay in his home, and said that if I need anything that someone else cannot organize, than I should come to him, so I want to find out what this big-mouthing is all about.

I take a tuk-tuk taxi to the bar where we met, and there he is, even sober. I am glad.

"Hi, African, good to see you again, what you up to? How long you stay? We need to go out tonight. Let me show you MY Bangkok!"

"Okay, great stuff, but business first. Let's sit at a quiet table."

We order Chang beers and sit. He's obviously a business man, and knows how to do it.

"What you need?" he asks. I say a passport. He sips his beer, and asks, "What else?"

"Oh, yeeaahh, sure. So tell me, can you organize?"

"Oh, my boy," he answers. "Takes four days and you have a Thai passport!"

"Oh no, no, that's not what I need. I was thinking of a South African one?"

"What for that? I thought you have one?"

"Yes, but it's not for me. It's for my best friend here."

"Okay. Never saw one. Well, what about a British one, wouldn't that do even better?"

"Hmmm, let me think. Yes... yes, will do. Can you organize?"

"Yes. I will have to use a friend, but I can't see a problem. It won't be cheap, though."

"How much, about?"

He makes a call, and speaks Thai for just a few minutes. Then he says, "It will take five days, and it's two thousand dollars cash, not negotiable!"

I know what that means, take a sip of my beer, and clash hands with him: deal!

I hand over an envelope with two pictures of Harun, and write down the details I wish to put in the passport. Place of birth changes from Johannesburg to London, everything else stays the same. He doesn't even ask what it is all for, which is fine by me.

"So, that gives you five party days. Where is your friend?"

I have to explain to him in short, where Harun comes from and who he is. My friend pisses himself laughing, boy, oh boy… hahaha. We have another beer, share some old stories, and promise to catch up again soon.

I enjoy an afternoon alone in downtown, buy some interesting books about sailing and boat building, and a few more cheap cell phones, which we will need later. Then I sit in a fancy bar, have another beer, and enjoy being here. I am proud of my plan, and how things have gone so far. Between my second and third beer, I try more cash machines across the road, and cash in another two thousand dollars, all in Thai currency. Lovely!

To exchange it for dollars with my German passport is no problem at all. It makes me smile that, even with all the money we'll spend every day here, we can still build up capital on the side. That is how I want it to be in the future: to either live off high interest, or to have a good business running, managed by staff. And then to just live life as I wish. What a beautiful world it can be, if one is out of the rat race of work, targets, appointments, reports and salaries. I treat myself to a two-hour massage, and take a walk back to our hotel.

Harun is asleep. How come? I don't have to worry. These girls won't steal or rip him off too much, since I always leave him only two thousand Baht. He doesn't really know our cash flow, and doesn't need to.

I study my sailing books at the pool, and have some beers, and enjoy the sun. He will spot me from the balcony if he wakes up. I will tell him again that he should never say where we come from, or where we are going. And he must definitely never say what we're going to do! He can take phone numbers and promise to come back, which he might do one day. So the answer to any question is that we are friends on a two-week holiday from London, where we work as accountants. That's it, full stop. I also need to teach him his new identity details.

Oh, there he is. Oh, my dear, what a beach bum! Colourful shorts, sun glasses, baseball cap, he's really adapted easily. Well, nothing difficult here with that, and he still does his praying.

"Cool, my friend. You already look like a new person, and it seems you will be British passport-holder in five days. Oh really, yes. I met a friend, and he's organizing it. It will cost two thousand dollars, and then we will leave here as soon as possible. In-between, we use the time to squeeze the credit cards to the limit, although we must live on a small budget here.

"Of course, we will still have lots of fun. My friend offered to show us Bangkok, which will be a different experience with someone like him. It might be hectic, but it will be big fun."

"I am ready for anything," Harun says. Yes, I believe so, now that he's had a taste of the sweet side of life.

So we spend the next day in leisure and are lazy, like we're on a real holiday, using the time for studying sailing tricks and gaining knowledge, and working on construction issues. On the side I make calculations for the equipment we need for our sabotage act.

I keep my notes short and clear, only understandable to me, but I have a fixed idea about how to build a projectile, installed in a trimaran, quite powerful, but also risky construction. We will need quite a big boat, to accommodate the load on the boat's body.

We have to get the load, which will be out of more or less pure TNT, out of the old land mines, stored in big volumes in Mozambique. There they are still clearing huge stretches of land, where big mine fields were laid during the war, but not registered or marked on maps. These days there is still farmland covered, and accidents happen daily, while locals try to farm for their daily food supply.

I'll never forget my first Mozambique experience in the fish market in the capital, Maputo. By chance, I'd met a chef from New Zealand in the backpacker where I'd stayed, and we got the idea to cook us a meal out of big Mozambique prawns. So we went to the market, and found the right size and quality, and, as every tourist does, we started to bargain for the price. Those days, one million Mozambican meticais were a thousand South African Rand, or about two hundred US dollars, so these high numbers irritated already. In ten minutes we'd managed to negotiate the price down by about only fifty cents, and the beautiful market girl wasn't happy at all, and, since neither of us could speak any proper Portuguese, it became more a game with the beauty. She could have been a model, with long, long black hair, bluish eyes, a gorgeous smile showing white teeth and skin like nougat chocolate; like a sister of Angelina Jolie.

Anyway, after we'd paid, it broke my heart when I saw the beauty, who'd been negotiating from a piles of boxes, jump down to the floor, to land not on her feet, but on the stumps of her knees, which were fixed and tied up with bits and pieces of old blankets. She disappeared, on hand and knees, into the masses of people in that dirty market hall. I couldn't believe my eyes; she was one of the mine victims and had lost both her lower legs, from the knees downwards. That's horrible. How much pain and suffering must she have been through, and we'd bargained for half an hour to save fifty cents. Shit, stupid us. I didn't enjoy the prawns that day; just couldn't forget the picture I'd seen: a beauty queen on her knees, damn it. It taught me a lesson, and

I've never bargained in these markets again. No, I always now pay a little more than was asked for. So yes, I do know the danger of the mines, but I also do know how to handle them,

If the detonator is out of the mouth hole in the middle of the mine, they are harmless. You can shoot into them, throw them in fire, and nothing will happen; it's just five kilograms of purest TNT! To bring it to explosion, you need a detonator, or a little electric capsule, which one can even activate with a cell phone call.

Its going to be a mission to get them, without awakening any suspicion, but I am sure I will find a way. For me, this undertaking is still the most complicated one of the whole plan, quite risky, but then again, I have good friends and contacts in Mozambique, and luckily we are not under time pressure to build our sailing bomb.

In the meantime, I've emailed to Achmeth in Mazar, using the email address he gave me, and as sender I used the other email address he'd set up for me.

I only mailed:

Hallo uncle, we are already quarter way, and looking forward to the firework at our arrival!

It took two days, and then he answered:

That is nice, take care. If you need pocket money after the arrival and fireworks, let me know where to send it.
Uncle Achmeth

Hmm. Okay, there is a clear message in it. At a later stage I will share my banking details with him, but at the moment it is not necessary to share more private details with him than he already has. But I set up internet banking for my Thai bank account, so that I can check the balance and any transfers from anywhere in the world. So far my Euro payment as caterer is untouched, thanks to the cash dollars from Harun's uncle, and there is the money that we have drawn so far. We've tried a higher amount from different cards every day, and by now we've already cashed in more than fifteen thousand dollars from the dead soldier's accounts, which we will, of course, pay back to his family after our mission is accomplished.

But today the machine swallows the Visa card; the banks don't always sleep. The Amex and Diner's go through again, letting us draw another two thousand dollars from each account. It is always like a little jackpot win.

I will meet Richy again later today, and hopefully get Harun's new passport. Unfortunately, we couldn't do the big night-life party with him. He went to Phuket to attend to business. Well, that's what he said. So far today I've only been able to get his voicemail, and I've already paid a thousand dollar up front.

I try all day, but still can't reach him. It gets me pissed off. What if he doesn't deliver? Shit, I'd never thought about that, but even then I will make another plan. Maybe he is just too busy.

Yes, he was. The next morning I get his SMS to meet him at the same place as before, and he blames me for leaving so many messages.

"Man, I took my Harley back from Phuket, and I don't answer calls when I am riding. Did you think I'd let you down?"

"Well, show me what you got."

He pulls a UK passport out of his bag. "Check it," he says, and throws it over.

"Damn, it looks good, quite real!"

"Oh, come on William, that one is *realer* than a real one! Hahahahah! Cheers!" and the beer bottles hit against each other. Waaoouuww, am I glad we got that done, more easily than I'd thought. I hope this gets us through customs.

"Don't worry, the document is clean, and registered in the computer system; and even got a stamp that you entered Thailand a few days ago, a perfect job."

Now my friend is not Harun anymore, now he is Brad. That was his wish, after watching some particular movies. Brad Cook is his whole name. This surname he also picked from the internet; the old sailor story of Captain Cook. Fair enough. I like his creative mind, it will be useful.

Now I can go and change the dates on our tickets to Kenya. Oh shit, damn shit, big mistake! How could that happen? How could I be that stupid? His ticket is still in his old name. Damn it. Well, it seems that there is nothing else to do other than to ignore it and get him a new one, in his new name. The whole of life is give and take, and we cashed in nicely here, thanks to the cards, and the well organized working of the American banking system.

It is June now, and nearly the rainy season, so it's a good time to go. We get a flight to Nairobi in two days. Everything is perfect so far, and we go off to a good restaurant, before we dig into the nightlife, Brad and William now. It took a while till he responded to the name, but after a few kicks under the dinner table, he's got sensitive to Brad.

After a rich and good meal, I lean back with a fine cognac and recall what is happening in my life.

This is all supposed to become a book. So far, we've had lots of fun, but we've also already done a few things that some people might call crime. We've got a faked passport, and have plundered someone else's bank account, and are in touch with the biggest terror organization of our time, and we are convinced that we will finish what we've started.

My Dad always said, even when I was a child, that my head is full of shit. How right he always was, but what I am going to do now would be too much for his imagination. I'm glad that nobody else really knows the details; even Brad is in the dark. All things considered, we are going to do something good, just in a very different way!

The next phase, on the African continent, will be a much bigger step, followed by a major sailing trip. I really haven't got a clue how to handle it, and the idea comes up to hire, in South Africa, someone experienced to do the Atlantic part with us, I will decide later, depending on budget. I've already got someone in mind who might do it for a small fee, but he should never get the true story behind the ocean crossing.

I go through my checklist before we leave this cheap country. Now we are properly equipped with cell phones, clothing and bags, music and books, even ocean maps that I got here quite reasonably, and, yes, we have Brad's UK passport. And, even after the expenses of this little holiday stop, we have nearly thirty thousand dollars in cash, already exchanged from Thai currency into US dollars, and my Euro salaries still untouched in my account.

I call this German efficiency, and I am looking forward to another good time in Africa.

On the last night in Bangkok, Brad didn't come home at all. I'd left him six thousand Baht to blow, and another test to see if I can leave him alone without him doing something stupid. And he didn't. He even reported back like a soldier for breakfast, with a long smile all over his face, no explanation needed. We take a taxi to the airport.

The test for his UK passport is coming up, and it goes nicely through, as well as my good old German passport.

Jambo Africa, we are coming. He behaves already like a regular airplane passenger. The first thing he does is to order two beers, which makes me smile. When I look at him, and I close my eyes afterwards, I can still see that bored boy with his chubby cotton coat sitting at his fire. Now there is a young man, full of positive energy, on a mission so special that I wouldn't know if anything similar has ever been planned by two men so different.

We enjoy our flight. All is going according to plan now. We won't waste too much time in Kenya. Depending on the airfares to Mozambique, we might even take an overland bus again, which will go through the most enjoyable scenery. Buying a car comes to my mind, but with a Kenyan number plate we will always be targeted by Mozambique authorities and thieves.

I have a good friend, who has access to all kind of explosives, living and working in Tanzania's capital. This would be worth an exciting drive across the country. I need to ask him for something little, six of them if possible. He must have access to new detonators for the blasting works in the mines under his control.

These detonators are half the size of a cigarette and, packed in the same sized box, I will carry them carefully till I need them.

I'd like to get us a base in Beira, in the north of Mozambique. It is one of the biggest shit holes on earth, but I have been there a few times and know how to get around there, and also how to get to my friends in Chimoio, a few hundred k's inland. I know where what we need is in Tete, north of Chimoio, a well known corridor and a hotspot in the previous civil war in Mozambique.

The construction of a boat and the organizing of the landmines will take some time. I need to check out the circumstance when there, and hope it will all go smoothly.

I calculate that we'll need at least six weeks in Mozambique. First, we need to find the right boat. This is very important. It must be the right size, and in good condition for the long sailing journey that will come next. We do need a safe place to build it. Maybe I can make a deal with the locals, to work where they build their beautiful traditional dhows. A dhow is a traditional Arabic sailing vessel, with one or more lateen sails. It is primarily used to carry heavy items, like fruit, along the coasts of the Arabian Peninsula, Pakistan, India and East Africa. Larger dhows have crews of approximately thirty people, while smaller dhows typically have crews of around twelve. There are smaller ones still, which a single man can handle alone.

I would love to try our plan with one of these, but it would get too much attention in the States. We need a normal, white trimaran, which won't get too much attention since there will be very many of that kind around.

JAMBO AFRICA

Kenyan Immigration is cool and fast. It seems they are happy with the fact that if one has a passport at all, they only need to concentrate on finding an empty page to press their stamp on, and they do that with a friendly: Welcome to Kenya!

I feel nearly home. I love to hear the English language around me, and I know we will have the best steaks here.

"Can't we stay at least a few days?" Brad asks. Did he read my mind?

Damn, why not? There's no reason to rush; every extra day gives me more time to think and plan. I remember a well known traveller lodge and campground right in the middle of town. An older lady started it more than thirty years ago, to give travellers passing through the capital a safe overnight opportunity, and, as it is in the travellers' world, the word got spread and by now it is a must-stay at least once. And gosh, how I love it, from the first moment we walk onto the property.

There are overland trucks from all over: German, Swedish, Dutch number plates, even an Austrian 2CV, and plenty of motorbikes.

We check in and get us the luxury of a room in the old villa.

I've never minded sharing a big room with a lot of other travellers, but now, with all our cash and stuff, I need a bit of privacy, to make sure I can hide our bits and pieces safely.

Then we go straight to the well-known meat place, where you can eat as much as you want, being served till you give a sign to the waiter not to serve more, like a *churasceria rodesio* in Brazil.

That, for me, is a paradise.

"And there are beautiful girls here too," Brad realizes.

"Yes, true, but here it is different. Thailand was a paradise, here it is more dangerous. Do not go with one. Talk, flirt and have fun, but do not go with them, promise!"

The long face from him is understandable. He had too much of a treat in Bangkok; any man can get used to that. I explained to him the saying, "Work hard, play hard"... now it is working!

After a mega-stunning feast we walk back to the campground. What an atmosphere. A few campfires are going. We look at each other, and start running towards the smell of fire, which we haven't had in the last ten days, and drop to sit at the fire, surrounded by cooking, talking, drinking, excited travellers from all over the world. These places are so important to visit when you travel here. You forward information from the places you have come from, and you get info for places you are going to, and that straight from the mouth of people who have just been there, so up to date. Too many times I've believed in my travel books, which were printed a few years ago. Here these meeting points are the information centre for overlanders and backpackers. The notice board in the hall is full of notes: people are looking for people, selling equipment, looking for a lift, and of course free internet is available close by.

Then there is a picture that catches my eyes: a lovely old Land Rover, almost the same version I drove in Afghanistan, just here the long version, and hey, it looks in the picture like it has a Mozambique number plate... ask for further info at reception.

I go straight there.

"Tell me about that red Landy. Can I see it?"

The girl calls another guy, and he says, "Yes, sir, come. We've had it locked in the garage for a month."

We go and have a look. Oh, how lovely. As rusty as the one I had, but with a Moz number plate – interesting – and equipped with roof carrier and tent, canister, winch and extra security locks. Yes, it is well prepared for a trans-Africa trip.

"What happened? Who and where is the owner?"

"It belongs to a British couple. They started with a Mozambique holiday, felt in love with Africa and bought the car, to drive across."

"And?"

"Well, the girl fell in love with a black guy here in Nairobi, so they split up, and left the car here and want to sell it."

"How much?"

"They're asking eight thousand dollars, but the engine's got problems, and now the car has already been standing for three months. All these travellers either already have a car, or don't have this money anyway."

Then the British guy joins us, such a white bread. I can read his disappointment in his face, such a dream-dancing, accountant type.

He is very excited, and swears to me how well the car runs, and says, well, that he needs the money urgently, to pay here and to fly back home to the UK.

I try to start the engine. Well, at least the starter turns, and the battery is charged. Then I open the bonnet. Waaoouwww, what is that?

I'd expected that little, four-cylinder Land Rover engine, and now, there in front of me is a lovely five litre V8 Mercedes engine, powered by a high-tech injection system, the kind that came out when I did my apprenticeship thirty years ago. I nearly smile, but being sometimes clever too, I make a long face, drop the bonnet, and say, "Oh, my Lord. With that kind of engine, nobody will ever help you here in the third world. Thank you," and I turn my back towards him.

A few seconds later he runs after me and says, "Well, I will be happy with six thousand dollars!" I keep on walking. He runs in front of me again. I stop, and offer five thousand dollars, and five minutes to accept or not!

"With that money you can fly home five times. At least! You got three minutes left!"

"But look, the tyres are nearly brand new, even the two spare tyres!"

"Two minutes!"

"Yes, but..."

I offer him my hand and give him a look in the eyes, no smile from me. He takes a deep breath, and our hands meet, deal done. He is happy, and I am too. Brad doesn't understand, I see that.

I grab him, and a six-pack of beer, and explain to him that he now owns a Land Rover, and that he will learn how to drive the car. I tell him that we will need a car in Mozambique anyway, and that we will need this kind of heavy engine in our boat, not necessarily to power it, but as a melted bullet, for when the explosives detonate.

Okay, too much info at once for him, but he understands that he will learn how to drive a car, and that's what counts for him. Will he maybe buy one of his dream cars after the mission is accomplished?

So, as I'd known, it is always worth it to visit these meeting points; one always gets what one needs.

This engine will get going better than it ever ran before, no doubt, and this car will do a good job during the construction and transport of equipment, and will allow us a lovely safari from here to Mozambique. Lovely.

Back at the campfire we enjoy our beers, and have chats left and right. I love this atmospheres, these backpackers are the real travellers, happy with the basics, mostly between jobs, or taking time off before they study, and mostly on a tight budget. And fearless! Seventy percent are usually girls travelling together, or even alone.

I remember them, when they arrived alone in the middle of the night at the backpacker in Chimoio, that I told them that, if I were their dad, I would give them a hiding. The answer was always, "Hey, come on, it was easy... nothing happened..." Yes, but there were those to whom something did happen while hitch hiking down from Malawi, and about whom we never heard.

We have a really nice evening, get a cool car, and finally sit at a fire again.

Next morning, before I pay for the car, I check something there and then in the engine. It is as I thought: there are, where the jets go into the engine, always rubber rings. If they get hard over the years, through the hot temperature of the engine, they burst, and the cylinder sucks too much air, which is not registered by the injection system. And then the engine doesn't start at all, or, runs badly, with little power, using far too much fuel. These rubber rings I will get here, in Nairobi.

This I do, not from the Mercedes dealer, but from an African plumber. He just cut them precisely out of an old tyre for me. Oh, how I love Africa!

By lunchtime the car is running smoothly and is tuned. Perfect. I am happy. Yes, what you once learned when young, you never forget. We take it for a test ride. Brad turns up the radio, but I need it switched off to listen for any funny noises. Exhaust, brakes all sounds good, and, with the Mercedes engine, it drives like a limousine.

Ok, a very good buy, and we will always be able to sell the chassis before we leave Mozambique. I get the papers from the British nerd, and pay him with Brad's uncle's filthy five and ten dollar notes.

"Sorry, but we worked hard for them," I tell him, and smile.

Ok, maybe it comes across as if I always tease the British a bit. It might be a reaction because of our history, and because of my experience of living and working in England, where they always tried to tease me with the old stupid saying: "Hey German, for you the war is over!"; and where I developed the answer: "Oh yes, and I am very sorry that you won the war. If you had lost the war, you would know how to build cars and sewing machines, and your wives would know how to cook!"

While we clean and fiddle on our Land Rover to get it ready, we are approached by two young Italian ladies. They've heard we are going to Mozambique? I give Brad a look, and he quickly hides his face and gets very busy cleaning the windows.

"Oh, you heard that? Yes... yes... we will eventually get there, why?"

"Well, we thought you might be able to give us a lift, and we can share the costs of petrol!"

"Hmmm... and you can cook, I guess?"

"Yes, sure, we make the best pasta you ever had!"

Brad seems damn excited. His window already shines like a diamond, and he hits the window hard by nodding, "Yes, yes," to me.

And what can I say? The way these two girls look, they must be family of Demi Moore. Can one say no? Chefs that support our petrol bill might be fun to have with us.

"Do you have a driver's licence?"

"Yes, of course."

"Okay, deal!"

My dear, here we go. I hope I'm doing the right thing. We could have got reasonable tickets to Beira, but here, with the decision to buy the Landy and go overland, my tummy talked, and my love for adventures in Africa. This I always wanted to do – to drive south from Kenya – and an inner voice might have spoken to me, telling me to do it now. One never knows if another opportunity will come up. Is there some fear in me? That all can go wrong or that we might end up somewhere locked up, or in a horrible accident?

"Stop it!!" Oh, there is Brad's voice again, and he did it again; he woke me up. "German," he calls me again, "don't be scared, all will be okay, and Allah is on our side."

"I fucking hope so!"

Then he throws me a beer. "Down it," he says. Lovely!

My brain doesn't stop. Now I have the money saved to start a normal business, in South Africa. It is an old idea, and I have been looking for investors for years. It's been a dream for a long time, and now I do this crazy thing! An absolutely crazy thing. So many challenges have poured into my life since I left Germany in 1990. I mastered them all, for the worse and the better, and, yes, I've risked my life before, but for much smaller results, and never for a sum of money that could change my life and allow me to realize the dream life I've wanted to have for twenty years. Hmm... and we spoke about it for months at the fire in Afghanistan. I know what irritates me, it's the cool life we have now. It relieves too much pressure. Here we are, with bags full of money, a cool Land Rover, two beautiful, very sexy girls, and sunshine and beaches! And yes, it won't last forever, so we need to finish what we started!

"Sir Brad, can you get me another beer, please?"

"Coming," and shhiiieep there it comes, flying over the car.

I know me. These phases come and go, that's quite normal, but I know also that we're going to do it. There is a bit of a devil in me that always makes me try the nearly impossible, and the imagining of what could happen to our life as a result of a successful mission is mind blowing.

We decide to give the girls a chance at test cooking this evening, and to get to know each other. I just have to have another briefing with Brad: we have to be in Mozambique in ten days at latest to start a voluntary job close to Tete. That's our story for our Italian babes.

Their cooking turned out to be fantastic, delicious, and we had plenty of beers and lots of red wine, and lots of fun...

Next morning, after coffee and tea - Brad can drink beer, but he runs away from coffee - we pack our stuff nicely in the car, say bye-bye to a lot of friends we've made, and drive out of the camp, direction south. Just on the highway, Brad throws in that we might have a stop in Mombasa, which is nearly on the way. The girls start screaming at the same moment, "Oh yes, we must go to the beach, just two days..." and Brad's eyes become glittering. Damn, every evening in the desert I promised him so much fun. Now, once again, I can't say no.

"Okay, but two days only. I don't know how the track is through Tanzania." And the music is turned up, and the beers go around, and, oh dear, the ladies are in their bikinis in the car. Lovely.

We arrive in the early afternoon. What a party drive. We had to stop twice to fill up with beer, but not once for fuel; the car goes like a sewing machine. Up north, we find a nice camp, with reasonable *rondavels*, right on the beach, I am just worried for the car, so I bribe the local security to stick to our car for two days; it's always worth it.

This seems to be a little honeymoon weekend. Brad moves, without any discussion, with Jessica into the one *rondavel*, and Danny grabs my bag and hers into the other. The cards have fallen. Beautiful, lets live it. I just take a chance and whisper into Brad's ear that he's not to fall in love, because I hate the movies where all is going smoothly, and then some woman, beautiful or not, fucks up the whole story.

I'm already a bit nervous, because now the two of us can't speak freely about what needs to be done. Well, let's call it another test. And, as I look at our catering team, it occurs to me that there won't be too much time for talk anyway. We are in a paradise, and there is my beach bum, Sir Brad.

"What's wrong?"

Okay, I got it. He swam in the dirty pond in the desert, in a lovely pool at the hotel in Bangkok, but here are four-metre waves, something new. Looking forward to our little sailing trip, he shouldn't be scared of anything about water, but he is. He can't even catch the beer I pass to him. In the end he has no time for fear, because one Italian at the left, and one on the right, grabs his hands and pulls him towards the waves. I am his friend and stick a few metres behind him, just in case. He seems a bit lost at first, definitely swallows some salt water, but he is too proud to show any weakness in front of the chicks.

Then, like a child, he gets into the movement of the water, and plays happily in the waves. I'm glad. If he were scared of the sea, it wouldn't be good.

We have beautiful days at the beach, even time to talk, while we send the girls shopping and cooking.

"Oh, William," he says, "I am so happy. I will be thankful forever to you. I feel reborn. Everything is nice and beautiful."

"Yes," I agree, "because we don't have to work, no early alarm clock, no stupid boss. This is a taste of how we shall live after our next pay-day from one of our uncles.

"And look, it's how I explained to you. One really doesn't need to be a millionaire. It's all about freedom, health, sunshine, food and fun."

"Yes, yes, yes, so right, and we will succeed. I don't want you to go back to stupid job. Neither can I imagine to be a shepherd again in the desert. We will succeed, because it is something good we do. We are not doing something bad, we do good, even if it will make bang. The message must be delivered, whatever it takes!"

Oh, isn't he cool? We are a match made in heaven. For a second I imagine the two of us in tuxedos during the next Cannes movie festival. Hahahha, but one never knows.

As usual, very good times always pass too fast, and we are already on the way to the Tanzanian border. Brad sits in front with me. I've told him it is better to watch me driving and to learn, but I actually couldn't stand it anymore that he was smooching all day with Jessica on the back seat. And so we've each got one lovely Italian hanging around our neck from the back seat. Lovely!

This border post is so typically African: filthy, no real running water, or useable toilets available, endless trucks stuck where papers are not in order, and hundreds of prostitutes trying to make a living. Their days might be counted already, when I read about the HIV infection rate here – about ninety percent.

I forget a twenty dollar note in my passport to speed it up a bit, since there is no proper proof of ownership to the car, other than the written contract between me and the British guy, and no insurance for the car either. And once in Mozambique, nobody cares as long one bribes with a few old dirty greens.($)

Now, even I enter an African country that I have never visited. It is time to do it, since it was once German East Africa, about a hundred years ago, and I like to spot the old roots of this. The capital must be another interesting filthy hole, where a friend from Johannesburg has his head office, as head of security for a number of mines. I am very sure that he can organize me something I need for my smart bomb.

It is a nightmare of a road, with pothole after pothole, each one deeper than the next. It is a very tiring driving. Too many people break, or even roll their cars on these roads. I remember the main highway from Maputo to Beira, where trucks and buses are laying on the side, left and right, and a lot of vehicles drive at night without lights, including the locals on bicycles. It's a suicide mission to drive at night.

We will not make it to Dar es Salam today, so I keep my eyes open for an overnight stop, not expecting too much. One of my passengers spots a sign to a lodge which sounds good to me, we turn into a small dirt road. Jack's Beer Farm, it says, 15km.

Well, then let us check out who Jack is. We find the place easily. There is a big security gate and I press the horn. Only seconds later a black chap opens it and lets us in. Then a white guy with a cowboy hat comes to welcome us.

He says, "Hallo, hallo, where you coming from?" but with a strong German accent. So I answer in German, and he starts laughing, "Oh man, haven't spoken German since weeks. Well, I haven't since four month now."

This is Jack, whose name is actually Konrad, but he is obviously a Jack of all trades. He is another proof that everywhere in the third world, in any jungle, in any desert, where one doesn't expect anything anymore, one finds a crazy German.

So, here he has a lovely renovated old farm house and some cute cottages. Brad takes over the check in, and, damn, he loves it. Well, we all do.

"Are you guys joining me for supper? I put a warthog on a spit." What a question, not only because I've had pasta for three days; warthog is the best meat on earth.

"Okay." He gives his black staff a sign with some local words. Then he asks if we want to try his home-made beer. Gosh, he's got it all to make me love him.

"Get me a bucket!" I shout and, laughing, we follow him into a barn. There it is, a little brewery, all self-made; some tanks, some huge pots to mix yeast and water and barley, tanks for further fermentation, a filter, and a system to fill kegs. There's no bottling line; what for? This beer one has to drink fresh, without any pasteurization. He gets each of us a half litre glass. It looks lovely, and smells great, and it tastes refreshing and pure. Lovely.

Wasn't it my first big dream to open a micro brewery somewhere in the African bush, to create a Mecca for all tourists, a beer branded after the legendary Big Five animals? Well, who knows, maybe these dreams will also still come true!

He definitely motivates me once again to do so. What a cool guy he is.

We sit around a fire and exchange stories, and he gives us some tips for the next part of our journey, and where to go in the capital. And the advice to leave the car locked at a hotel for the time we are there. There is too much mugging and stealing in this crowded city. He only goes there if he really has to, otherwise he sends his staff if he needs something.

With some new useful information, and after lots of fresh beer, we enjoy the lovely, juicy *spitbraai*. This meat is out of this world. Once I have my own farm in Africa, I will have a *spitbraai* at least once a week, and invite all my friends. The meat and beer makes us tired, and we still need some fun. "Good night, Jack, thanks for everything."

Next day we have an early breakfast, as good as dinner was the night before. We pay him for the great service, exchange email addresses, and are back on the road, back on the potholed track. After four hours we reach the outskirts of Dar es Salaam, township all over, as it is in all the poor African countries, with locals walking and carrying heavy loads on both the left and right of the road, going from nowhere to nowhere, trying to make a living with a little something. It is a tough life, but these people live like ants, and always survive. They're not like the thousands of Americans and Europeans who went bankrupt in the last recession, where people even committed suicide because they lost millions of their billions. How weak and dumb is that? The people here have nothing to lose other than what they are wearing. They have no stocks, no shares – but they always seem to have a cell phone. I always wonder where they charge them.

We make use of a little map Jack has drawn for us, and find a guesthouse, also run by a German, this time an old farmer, I'd guess far above the eighty-year mark; a walking dictionary about African history.

Luckily, I never delete any phone number in my South African handy. I give Trevor a call, and, lucky again, he picks up after only one ring.
"Hey mate, it is William here, from Hermanus!"
"Damn, buddy, where are you?"
"I hope close to you!"
"What, are you here in Dares? Great stuff brother, time to meet?"
"Yes, where and when?"
So we make a meeting point. I will see him alone, and organize a sightseeing tour for the others. Business comes first for me. This meeting is very important. I do need the right ingredients, and

am damn sure he can get them, although I'm not going to tell him what for.

I meet him an hour later in a dingy pub in down town. It is always good to see old friends, and he is one of a kind. He's had a career as a body guard and security specialists, he has shot two guys during bank robberies in Johannesburg, he doesn't take shit, but unfortunately can't go back to South Africa for various reasons.

Of course, he asks me what I am doing and I make up a bit of a story, just because it is shorter to. I tell him I will help a friend to build a lodge in Mozambique, in the mountains, where he has to blast some rocks, to get a road built. This crazy guy likes to do this with mines he's cleared on his property, but doesn't know how to do it, so he's asked me for help, knowing about my past in the army.

"He sounds like fun. How can I help you?"

"Well, I need a few of these little electric detonators one screws or sticks into the landmines!"

"Oh, that shit! Yeah, they are dangerous. Handle with care!"

"Yes, I know how dangerous they are. Never forget the special pliers we had to use in the German army, one kilo of iron, to press the normal detonator capsules on blast cable, and then, in my last month of service in the Foreign Legion, they made us bite them together with our teeth. Fuck, I have never been that scared."

Trevor pisses himself laughing. He can imagine that.

"How many do you need?"

I remember that they come in boxes of eight; such a box will do.

"Shouldn't be a problem, that I can organize, but not today, it is Sunday, but tomorrow, on Monday, no problem."

Good stuff, what a relief for me to get these things here.

Then he keeps talking about the mine clearing in Mozambique, that it is a never-ending story, that most of them are deeper than one imagines, and that after every rainy season, mines are washed up again, and new fields are found. But it is a forgotten project for the outside world; too many new wars all over.

"Nobody pays or educates the locals on how to clear them. You would be the right chap to do something for Africa!"

"What do you mean?"

"Well, I know the right person in charge. Make an offer to them to educate the locals about these mines, and how to clear them without danger."

Gosh, my boy, you've just got my biggest problem solved. That is the way I can get to my main ingredients, of course.

"Hey, where are you?" he shouts.

"Oh, I was just thinking about what you said. It is fine with me, if they pay me well."

"You damn German, there is nobody that pays you for that. It is voluntary work. Don't be so stingy, help these people!"

I think again of the beauty queen, Angelina, from the Maputo fish market.

"Okay, I can do that. I have an open end here, nothing really serious in the pipe line. I've got a few weeks spare. Cheers!" and I order more beer, while he starts writing some names and numbers down. Then we chat a bit about life here. He earns well, has married a local, and has five kids... goodness me, well done!

Then we make an appointment for the next morning, and I get back to meet the others at the guesthouse. I laugh about how things are falling into place. Even though it is a dangerous job to clear mines, it can be done safely, although very slowly. It will give me the best opportunity to charge our boat with the explosive stuff. I just have to harvest it; it's as easy as that.

Here are my tourists, happy little shits, all of them, hanging at the pool, and little Prince Brad enjoying it the most. If his uncle could only see him now.

I order a beer and have a dip in the pool. I'm really relieved. This meeting was very important for the success of the whole mission. There will be a need for detonators to clear some of the landmines too. One can do the dangerous part, and unscrew the detonators, or one can just blow them up.

Trevor had mentioned, however, that all black authorities in charge sold the stuff to Zimbabwe, to Robert Mugabe's rebels. Well, at least I have some contacts there, who can point out where landmines are, and damn sure they will know stories about the mine clearing there in the past, and then I'll take it from there.

The four of us enjoy another great evening. Yes, we really have fun. It's cool: two couples without any issues, just happy and enjoying the moment, living life. I love it.

We have an early breakfast once more, and at ten I go to meet Trevor again, this time in his office. After a handshake, he opens a safe and gets me a box of detonators. I can't believe what I see. they are still sealed, and made in the old eastern Germany. I hope they will work.

He shows me one from an open box. It is more or less the same as the west German ones I know, with a metre of cable at the end, perfect.

"What do I owe you?"

"Another visit, my friend, after you've cleared some mine fields," he says, and he makes me laugh. That's a kind deal. He's got work to do, and I've got to go. "Cheerio, my friend, and please, this stays between us!"

"Hey, what you think brother?" and he kicks my bum. Thanks again.

INTO MOZAMBIQUE

So we're back in the mud, after a heavy rain at night. We need to be even more careful, but it gets dry after a few hours. I am excited. I will finally test a new border post right at the coast, into northern Mozambique. They only opened it in 2007 on demand from nature conservation, and hunters, and authorities, since poachers from Mozambique move illegally into Tanzania for big game. I also remember that any entrance into Mozambique is always a hassle, so I keep some bigger greens ready.

This is a lovely scenic drive, with high trees and lush foliage. We even see animals, buck and zebra, kudu and endless monkeys of all kinds. The kids – I mean Brad and the girls – are speechless. We take some wrong turn offs that end in the middle of nowhere, but there are really no signs, and it is difficult to see what is the main road and what is the turn off. Oh, I just love Africa. Then we are stopped by a boom, a border post smaller than any private security entrance in the luxury parts of Sandton, a fancy suburb to the north of Johannesburg.

There are two officials, one even in uniform and armed. They must be bored to death here, and there are only two, to keep each other company. On the side, in the bushes, is a *vrot* tent, where they most probably live.

One of them points with his rifle that we have to leave the car, which we do, and then he searches all over, time waster. Finally, he takes us to the little cabin, where his colleague, or comrade, is waiting and waiting, with the stamp already in his hand. There are two Italian, a German and a British passport, kind of entertaining for him. He asks in Portuguese if we are not married, that much I understand. I answer no… not yet… and smile.

Then he opens each passport and gets angry, shouting, "Visa, visa!"

I play stupid – it's something I can do easily and it helps a lot sometimes. I try to explain to him that he will give me the visa, that I believe this is his job, and that he gets paid for this. He makes it clear that he doesn't get paid enough.

Wife and seven children? Sure, sure, I know. So isn't it good that we bring him business? We need four visas now, and I ask in a friendly way if he would like a beer. It is very humid and hot. I've prepared Brad to bring a six-pack for us, and so he does.

He starts smiling, and now I tell him that I've got friends waiting in Pemba, and that I am kind of in a hurry, not knowing how bad the road will be. I am already a bit drunk so I realize only now that one of them is a Mozambican, and the other guy is the Tanzanian official, so both need some pay. We argue and discuss a bit, even say we'll drive back and take another way and walk away, but he calls us back and, after an hour, we've each got our visa for fifty US dollars in cash. That is more or less the normal price, and by now he has already had three beers and doesn't even ask for any documents for the car.

Thank God and Allah, happy people are always lucky! We cross a little river which marks the border, and we are in Mozambique. A new phase can begin, but we might also have to say bye-bye to our girls very soon.

I put foot. I want to get to Pemba, another really funny end of the world, with a huge, famous campground, run by an Australian. It's a good place to hang out, and check boats. Maybe I might even make a sailing course.

The north of Mozambique is very dry, but beautiful, with stunning beaches and lots of mystery islands in the front of its coastline. The best is Ibo Island, a place where the time stands 250 years before, on the roots of the old Portuguese fort built hundreds of years ago, and used as a prison during the civil war. Today, fishermen still catch human skeletons in their fishing nets.

There are even some five star resorts at Pemba. It is all about diving, and kite surfing now in this area. The streets are dirty and dusty. There are no really good shopping centres for food and stuff, but somehow one gets it all if one looks for long enough. I'm fairly sure that I'll eventually find the boat that I want.

We arrive at the campground, which has changed quite a bit since I was there four years ago. He's built a lot more, and the place is quite busy.

People – residents and locals from the area – love the daily dinner buffet, and all kind of funny creatures meet up there for sundowners. There are dingy looking hunters, all with 4x4s with South African number plates, and this is a good area for outlaws, to hide and dive.

We decide on one of the lovely two-bedroom cabins, since the Italian ladies love the place too, and they only have ten days left before they need to get a return flight from Maputo.

Pemba also has a lovely coastal stretch, with restaurants and night clubs, places to be careful, places where they put drugs in your drinks and, as I said, there are lot of outlaws around, and I feel responsible for Brad and the girls. At least I get around with my bad Spanish here. The others are pretty stuck because hardly any Mozambican speaks some English, only a few youngsters, who go regularly to school, or who work as a tour guide for foreigners, showing them where to shop, and where to get a ferry. Like everywhere in the world, one needs to be very careful with the guys that offer their services on the street; you never know where they might take you!

The next morning I receive an email from Uncle Achmet:

"I hope you are enjoying the journey, and have not forgotten our party?"

I answer:

"My dear uncle, how could I forget the party? I am dreaming of it every day, and will be there in time!"

Here, on the magic beaches, it all turns into holidays again and why not? So long as I get my research done during the day, and keep on writing what has happened so far, because, at the end of the day, it was the main idea to write a book. Now I am impressed by how it is to live it, and how details come together.

I observe the locals to see how they build the dhows. I'd like to have one later, just to cruise the whole Mozambican coastline with friends. It is mostly still untouched; turquoise blue sea with fantastic coconut-tree-lined beaches – and lots of goats in-between. Brad loves it. He is smiling at them. Sure, there must be memories coming up, but these days he is collecting new memories by the minute. He and Jessica are like a couple. He feels like a man, taking her to the beach to swim, having beers. He has to catch up on a lot of what he's never experienced in his previous life.

We also book a day trip with a trimaran, to the neighbouring islands. When we go, I am very curious about how the boat will go, and how much action and effort it is to control it. I stick to the skipper, asking him endless questions.

Yes, that's the kind of boat we need. It got lots of space in the middle for our main... well, main what? Let me call it cannon for now. We need a slightly smaller one, with not too much high tech equipment and no luxury. I will put in the Mercedes engine from our car, firstly to power it if we get into trouble or out of wind, and later, once at our destiny it will serve a more important purpose.

The plans for our cannon are keeping me busy. I would love to ask some comrades, who are sitting around Kabul as majors, for advice but the questions I've got are better not discussed on Facebook. I do my formulas, as every technician did in the old days – a bit more of that, stronger here, to insure full function, and maximum results if needed!

While the others relax at the beach, I hang about in the marina, off a little yacht harbour. There are a few freaks, with boats that they have built by themselves. They either run a charter business, or are on a trip around the world. It is easy to get into conversations and to pull out information about the route, what the problems are and so on, but more importantly, about how to build, what the main criteria for building a safe boat are.

It seems that the first thing is weight – there should be nothing that you do not need. I'd thought so, and am already calculating up and down. We will need water, food, petrol and at least one and a half thousand kilos of ingredients for the cannon. Sometimes I need a double whiskey to wash my thoughts and worries down. Oh, my Lord, under what frustration and depression did I develop this crazy plan, the challenge of my lifetime?

What is important now is to get a trimaran. I wish there would be another crazy British man, whose girlfriend went off with a black guy, and he had to sell his boat. Wishful thinking! I just need to keep my ears and eyes open, and I will find what is needed.

If not here, then later in Beira, or even in Vilanculos.

At least it relaxes me at the moment that our cash is okay. Life here is cheap, the food is good, there's plenty of sunshine, and we have nice company. And every day I make new contacts that bring me a bit closer to my goal.

On the internet I study trimarans. The kits one can buy, and build up, are not cheap at all, and there is no way to order a new one anyway.

After a few days, I meet two couples from New Zealand. They have just arrived and need to find out how to get around. I tell them what I know, as they asked me, and a good talk starts, There is always a quick connection if you are German, and when they hear your accent they tell you that their grandfather was German. Oh, damn. How interesting is that supposed to be for me?

But then it does get interesting very soon, because the second couple had the same trimaran as the first, but there had unfortunately been a gas explosion, and the whole boat burned out. All the equipment and computer, the air-conditioner, all this important shit that I wouldn't need anyway was burned. I play the same role as when I bought the Land Rover.

"Oh, my dear, so it is just an empty shell, most probably with cracks all over?"

"Yes, the explosion popped the boat against the jetty in Beira, and two old iron bars from there stuck right through the main body. It's a wreck now, and will need months of restoring, and there is nothing to get here. We only pulled out of our jobs for five months. We want to sail, and experience that. We've no time to build a boat on a beach here."

"Okay, I understand. That's tough." My tummy is already laughing inside me. "So what're you going to do now?"

"Well, so far we're getting along together on one boat. It's a bit tight, but at least we can go ahead with our journey as planned."

Fair enough. One doesn't often get so much time to do such a trip.

"And what about the wreck?"

"Well, the insurance paid, luckily, so we left the wreck in Beira."

"You just left it? Just like that?"

"No, it is chained and locked up, but we couldn't find anyone interested in it." "The locals might move in with ten people and live in it." I add.

Oh yes, they would. If you could see how they live with thousands in the old Grand Hotel in Beira, which was once the best hotel on the African continent. The owner ran out of money, and the locals just took it over, slowly but surely, as a township on its own, with hundreds of open cook fires on the balconies, and hundreds of miles of washing lines all around it; a picture like in a Mad Max movie.

My brain is spinning. This is exactly what I was looking for, and it is already in Beira. An empty shell is exactly what I need, burned out or not, as long as it swims, and has got space.

"Look guys, I will start a voluntary job close to Beira, and my dream was always to build my own boat, but I've never had the capital. I'd already planned to fix up a dhow, and sail with it to Europe after my job!"

"Oh, my boy," the grey-haired skipper says, "you will kill yourself. I wouldn't put my foot on such a nutshell!"

"Well, I am not that fussy. If the locals can, then I can. But I hear what you're saying. A well-designed, professional boat such as yours was, would be much safer and better. I trust you with that, sir!"

"I tell you something. If you have eight thousand dollars to spare, you can have it, and do what you want with it!"

Oh, what a greedy bastard. He got paid by the insurance, and still wants more. Then his wife steps to my side.

"Well," she says, "if you are really interested, you can have it for six thousand dollars. That's the balance between what we invested, and what the insurance paid, and we will transfer it into your name on its papers."

Great, even though the last favour is not necessary: better not. That sounds like a deal: six thousand dollars for a burned out shell, the same amount I will ask back for the Landy when we leave.

"Okay, guys, sounds fair to me. I will need to save from my little voluntary salary to get it fixed up, but at least it's a great start. Thank you, guys. But I would like to see it, before I give you my last savings. Please let me speak to my friends, and I'll catch up with you for a sundowner later." I shake hands, and off I go, whistling happily like anything. That's another headache less. If the burned out one is the same as the one they arrived in, then it's the perfect size and shape.

I want to see it as soon as possible and secure it, before it gets recycled by the locals in Beira; they might build three huts out of it, that's Africa. I have to pull Brad away from the girls, and tell him the news. He is fascinated too, knowing that I had a headache over the issue of where and how to get a reasonable boat.

Now I am thinking, shall I quickly fly there and sort it out, so Brad can pay the owners here after he got my okay, and then he can drive down with the girls alone? Hmmm...not a happy thought for me. Okay, I will fly alone to Beira, and fly back to here, to sort out papers and payment, and then we can all drive down to Beira together.

That plan is fine with Brad. I manage to book on the evening plane, and promise to be back the next day. I share the same plan with the guys from New Zealand, and have a quick two beers with them, and then go off to the *aeropuerto*. It is a nice flight. I always wonder how the locals can afford these overpriced tickets, but at this time it shouldn't be my problem.

My thoughts are with the boat, so I don't even care that I am ripped off by the taxi driver, who takes me from the airport to the jetty where the wreck is supposed to be. I run up and down the beach, and then I spot it, lying half on the side. It seems to be filled with quite a lot of water, which at least kept the locals from stealing it.

Then a boy approaches me. They told me they had chosen a friendly street kid to keep an eye on it, and paid him for two weeks in advance, and he is still here! Sometimes, Africa is full of surprises, but I must say that we are just a bit damaged here because the negative experiences are unfortunately more than the good ones.

This boy can be quite useful in future. I tell him that my friends have sent me to check on him and the boat, and that I am glad that both are still here, and give him another twenty dollar note. After this I ask his name, Clifford it is, and I introduce myself.

Then I spend more time around the wreck. The smell of fire, melted plastic and copper cable is still strong. The mast is okay, The sail is burned, but that can be replaced locally. Each hole, big and small, in the body can be fixed with fibreglass patches, no problem at all. Then I see its name shining through the clean shallow water. It is difficult to make it out. It starts with Wa... Walk...the...Talk! *Walk the Talk*, what an interesting name for a boat.

I am happy with what I see so far. It is worth the asking price, and at this point we can still afford it. I walk down to the lovely beach pub, a huge thatched building and, I would say, the best pub in Mozambique, a meeting place for all Zimbabweans who come to the coast for a holiday and fishing. It serves nice draught beer and good steaks.

I call the owner of the boat and verify the funny name, and ask why they called it so? I'm told that it is because their dream to build a boat was about ten years old, sometimes forgotten, sometimes freshened up, but then, when Sean became a pensioner and got bored at home, he said, "Let's do it and build it and sail the world, Walk the Talk!" And they did it. Hmmm, quite funny that it's already experienced one explosion. Very funny!

Walk the Talk! Our boat!

I down the first beer with a big smile. "Okay guys, then I'll see you tomorrow."

After the best steak for a while, I walk down the surprisingly well-looked-after promenade. I remember that there were a few guesthouses down there, and it seems that the ladies of the night know that as well, as they are all over and looking for business, which they won't find with me. I want a good sleep, and to be up early in the morning, to get the nine o'clock plane back to Pemba where my chauffeur Brad will pick up his Captain William.

I love things to be organized. Once a German, always a German.

And so it happened. I give him a big hug, and tell him how happy I am about what we've got, and that we have a big job to do, and that we still have to find a safe place to rebuild and equip our boat, which shouldn't be a problem at all.

We enjoy a last day at the beach in Pemba. The plan is to drive to Beira in the morning, after the paperwork is sorted, and payment is made. We meet the New Zealand couple in the morning, and sort it all out before we hit the road.

The road is a nightmare again, although there is no traffic at all. Why would there be? There is really nothing going on between Beira and here; the north is the poorest stretch of Mozambique,

In the west they've got the farms, run by mostly poor Zimbabwean farmers who were kicked out by Mugabe, and who started under big promises all over again, in the country they'd fought against during the civil war, now white refugees in the same country, knowing that they might get ripped off again by the local authorities too. They have, however, no choice. Some have even lost their wife and kids, who relocated back to their family homes in England. The hard conditions in this poor African country are not for a spoilt lady.

We cruise slowly and comfortably down, enjoying sound and beer as usual. The girls are very quiet, knowing they will leave us in Enchope, at the big junction between Beira and Chimoio, from where they have to catch a bus to Maputo. I hate this bye-bye-saying between travellers, after one has spent so much good time together. At least these days one can stay in touch via email and Facebook. When I travelled to South America twenty years ago, one exchanged postal addresses, and maybe one wrote one letter; but then, one lost contact.

With the promise to stay in touch, and to surely meet again, we hug each other goodbye, and now it is only Brad and me again: the two guys, on their big mission.

BEIRA, BOAT AND MINES

I show Brad the wreck, and introduce him to Clifford. Then we sit on the lovely verandah at the pub, eat steaks and drink beer, looking over to *Walk the Talk*.

We need to get the boat out of the water, which we can do with the Landy and the winch, but we do need a trailer, at least for one day, to take it somewhere protected from other people's eyes, a safe place for at least a month. There is no better place to find out about opportunities than this pub. And we don't even have to make up a story. We just want to restore the boat, and sail around Africa, that is something a lot of people do. What we intend to do later it is in nobody's interest to know.

Our luck holds. We hear about a farmer who has a huge property here, with plenty of watch dogs, but he has to go to England for a while, to try to sell property there, in order to have funds for his farming project here. If we look after his house and dogs, then that would be wonderful. There is even an old lady who can cook and wash. Lovely!

We share lots of stories again, and realize that we have some friends in common in Chimoio. I enquire how they all do, exchange some phone numbers, and we have plenty of laughter and beers, and follow the friendly farmer to his property the same evening, where we spend the first night in our roof tent. In the morning, he makes us familiar with the house, and shows how to get water out of the waterhole if the municipality pumps go on strike, which usually happens here in Mozambique at least once a week. Then he gives us a whole bunch of keys, for an endless number of padlocks and other locks.

That's Mozambique. Everything needs to be locked up. The locals eat nails, and even drink paint, as the farmer says. His five dogs are quite something, mixed breeds between Boerboels and Rhodesian Ridgebacks. These dogs were used to hunt Lions! Any more questions?

Brad is not very happy with them being around. Sure, he enjoyed Jessica and Danny more. We hope that we will get a call later to hear that they arrived safely in Maputo.

Richard, the farmer, even calls a friend, who he is sure will help us out with a trailer. Great stuff, that is how I know Africa. If you don't know someone who can help, you will find someone who knows someone who can help. Farmers help each other; not only in South Africa's old Boer war, where ten thousand farmer fought a quarter of a million British soldiers, a hundred years ago. These guys are tough, like biltong and camel-thorn wood.

Our job for today is to get the boat out of the water. I hope there is not any more big, hidden damage. Richard's friend does not only lend us his trailer. No, no, he will not leave us alone with this mission, and points out exactly where we have to place the trailer. But, before we can winch it onto the trailer, I first have to pull the boat away from the jetty with our winch, while thousands of litres of water runs out of plenty of holes. When it is out of the water, I can't see any further big damage.

We will rinse it at the farm to get the salt off, and let it get dry in the sun before we start working on it. We are happy now, and we have a campfire on the farmer's big property. I look around at what we've got. There is a Land Rover with a Mercedes engine, and a boat, ready to build as a swimming cannon. Yes, there's quite some work to do, but that kind of work is fun for me.

Brad is shaking his head. It is not even a month since we left Afghanistan, but what he's experienced so far is still unbelievable to him.

"And you lived already twenty years like this?" he asks me.

"No, not as good as this. I always had my jobs to do, and I never had such a sexy car, and so much cash available. Come on, so far we are on a holiday.

"But tomorrow our work starts. After we've stripped the boat of all the burned bits and pieces, we need to check each detail we have to fix. Then we need to find out where we get the materials here – not to forget our voluntary job. I might have to attend that alone, it might be better and safer, at least at the start. But don't worry, I will keep you busy on the boat! Please forget about the girls who follow us since we moved in here. Playtime will be over for a while. Now it is hard work."

Yes, I think I will let him do the cleaning of the wreck, and the sanding around the holes, while I go out in the direction of Chimoio and make contact with the people who cleared landmines up in Tete. That issue gives me the next headache. I do not want to get blown up by a forgotten landmine there, and I do not want to chase badly educated, money-hungry, small-brain locals into the mine fields, and to deal with big casualties and accidents.

I need to get there, and check. The situation might be all bullshit, but better that it's not. These mines have been lying there now for more than twenty years. They might be more dangerous than they were when new. The TNT will still be okay, even though there is probably some dangerous fluid being produced inside, as happens when the stuff gets old; like old cheese when its been around for too long.

The wreck is dry next morning, and Brad can start to strip and clean it. It seems that we've got a little helper; Clifford is pressing his face to the gate. The dogs are going mad, but he is not scared at all. I guess he got used to barking dogs while living as a street kid. Of course, he had a job watching the wreck. Now it is behind gates, and there is nothing for him to do, but he can keep Brad company while I am gone, and help as well as he can, Brad is fine with that. Me to, so I leave them alone and hit the road. It should be four hours to Chimoio. The road is bad as usual, and the kids are selling lobster on the side; very delicious, as long as fresh – I mean the lobster. But no time for that now.

I can think and concentrate best when driving a car. The main brain is on the street, and the other part gets creative. It is more than twenty years ago that I had a mine in my hand, but the ones used here will be more or less the same as those I am educated in.

Each of them was usually five kilo's heavy. I will need at least three hundred of them to make one and a half tonnes of TNT. That should do what I want it to do, but will be quite some weight – another reason to leave all other luxuries off the boat. I'll need to do some measurements on the boat, but first I need proof that I can get them.

In Chimoio I go straight to the Italian Pub, usually very well visited by the Zimfarmers. And that's the case: a lot of familiar faces, but a lot of them I don't want to waste my time with. There is just one; he is a guy who works partly for the government, and partly for the tobacco industry. He knows all the land reforms and claims, since he is in charge of the relocated farmers and their land, and he will have more info about the mine fields which are still left.

He remembers me well. Yes, we've even got common friends back in South Africa.

"What you doing here? Long time no see. How is Brigitte?" I knew that question would come.

"Sorry, Paul, I saw her only once since we got back from Thailand, and I've no idea where she is now." I want to change the subject quickly, and get to the point, but he's already asked what I am up to here in this shithole. So true.

"Well, I met guys who worked voluntarily for a project, where they actually cleared landmines."

"Oh!" He starts laughing and spits out his drink, and lifts his half arm. "You want to look like me? Or even worse? Why the fuck you want to do such shit job, which can kill you any second!"

"That's the reason I am here, I want to have a look at the project and area, to see what the situation is, what the equipment is, and so on."

"If there is a way I can help, I will do so. Okay, where is it? Behind Tete?"

"Yes, that's what I have been told."

"I do know that there are plenty of mines lying around, but I can't recall an active project anymore. There is no finance for that, and by now the fields are fenced in, so there are only one or two accidents every year, when people try to win another few square metres for farming, shit happens. These days, there is even an old American veteran involved. His name is Mac. He is still around, and grows his own tobacco now on a small farm. Have a chat to him," and he gives me his number. That sounds like a good contact.

We finish the talk with how his wife and kids are, and life in total, clap shoulders, and, see you around, take care, off I go.

I jump straight into my car, pay the watch boy, and head in the direction of Tete. Seventy k's before the city, I fill up with petrol and give Mac a call – only voicemail. I wonder if he has signal on a farm. I leave him a message to call me back, and drive ahead. Before I hit the horrible town of Tete, he calls me back and asks me to give him a call back now; airtime is so expensive.

Okay, I do. I tell him who I got his number from, and who I am, and what I want.

He calls me an idiot straight. He says I should go back to where I come from, and get a life. Nobody voluntarily clears mines anymore, what for?

"That's a Russian roulette which you will lose sooner or later, my boy! you must be mad! Don't waste my time," he growls, and he drops the call, damn it, and then, despite several attempts, he doesn't pick it up again.

Drives me mad, but what now? Well, I keep on driving, checking the surroundings. It's the same scenery as everywhere here; men are carrying charcoal, either on foot or on overloaded bicycles. They've made it by chopping the last trees around them. Woman are carrying washing and water on their heads, and most have got a child tied onto her back, and one or two children are escorting their mum. There is nothing else for them to do: no toys or TV, just the daily procedure to get going.

I stop at a stingy street restaurant. Here I only stop where I can keep an eye on my car.

I need a beer to think. There wasn't any useful information from the American, not even an idea where mines can be found. He was actually right. What healthy, halfway intelligent man would risk his life to clear that craziness of mines, a life threatening gamble by the second? Where he is right, he is right.

Hmmm... that guy might be short on cash, considering that he asked me to give him a call back. I want to see him and have a long talk. I call him again, but get only voicemail. I leave him another message.

"Hi Mac, it's me. Please answer my call. I need to try your tobacco. Heard it is the best in the country. I could swop it for a few bottles of Scotch I brought in from Tanzania, if you are interested. Well, just a thought. Please let me know. I will still be around for an hour!"

Every old American loves Scotch, and I know how bad the supply is here, and how expensive, and if someone doesn't have airtime, then his bar must be nearly empty. It takes not even ten minutes, and I get a *please call me* message.

Smile... So he likes whiskey. I call him, and he confirms immediately that his tobacco is the best in the country, that's quite right, and he's still got some stock I could buy.

"Sounds great. Where can I try it?"

"Hmm... you got some whiskey with you?"

"Yes, a box of six bottles. I was going to give it to my farmer friends."

"Well, I don't have much time, but pop in for a tasting. We might make a deal."

I agree and get directions on how to find him, as I do an hour later. After lots of bad tracks and stony driveways, there it is a cosy little hut, a bit fucked up from the outside, but nicely placed on a little hill with a stunning view. He looks as I imagined him. He must be around eighty. He's already got two glasses waiting for us. That's a good situation for me: I will get my information. I pour us some good Scotch.

I actually bought it at the huge supermarket in Chimoio, the biggest Checkers Supermarket in Mozambique, I believe, but guess he never leaves his farm to go further than to the closest little Indian grocery market. He downs the first whisky, and pushes the glass over to me, smiling, already quite friendly, while I pour another one for us.

"So, where is the tobacco?"

He is now convinced that I really have whisky, and he runs into the house, and comes back with a wooden box. Inside are dark brown cigarillos. The smell coming out of the box is fantastic. He stretches the box out to me, and shouts, "Only one, Mister!"

"Of course. Only one. Then that is your last whisky, I think..."

So there we sit, smoking what is probably one of the best cigarillos in the world, and enjoy a good Scotch. Then he picks up the other issue again.

"Look, my boy, you need your both hands – one to smoke, one to drink – and your legs to be able to get a regular supply. You look healthy and happy. Why would you want to risk your beautiful life to clear this shitty land here?"

I slow down and say that I wanted to have a look at it, since I've never seen a real minefield, and that I want to write about it, and maybe get some attention from the first world, to establish another big project, to clear all the left-over mines. Waaouuww, this cigar gets my fantasy going.

"Okay, that's a good thought behind it," he says. "That would be wonderful, because you need big machines, diesel and maintenance. You can't do it anymore, like they did straight after the war, sticking long metal sticks into the ground, knowing they are two inches max under the soil. Now they've all moved. Twenty years worth of rainy seasons has shuffled these mines everywhere.

"Twenty years ago they cleared hundreds a day, and had daily casualties. It was a mess, worse than in the war, but as they paid the locals for every mine cleared, you can imagine how they searched, and disrespected the safety rules!" He pushes his empty glass over to me, and he gets another Scotch.

"But now tell me, where is this mine field from here?"

He shakes his head and grumbles, "You really don't want to know," and downs his whiskey, but yes, I damn well do want to know, I need to know.

He passes over his glass again, but I hold it tight, and ask him slowly, "Where are these minefields?"

He only points with his finger at his glass. Okay, one more, and then he starts talking.

The minefields are left and right along the main road, after the bridge when you leave town in a northerly direction. During the war, they had to protect this bridge as well as possible, in order to keep the access to the south, so every little pass across the mountains is full of mines – cheeky personnel mines and anti-tank mines – but you can imagine how the hills get washed down during every rain and so mines collected in the valleys and are grown over by plants again, till they move in the next rain. Some even explode when they get hit on their lid by a stone. And those that were secured to the ground when they were placed also detonate when washed away by heavy rain. That's scared most of the locals away, and has made it forbidden territory. The locals would love to use the land for farming, but too many have died on this land.

"It's not worth the risk," he says. "Trust me. By now, twenty years after the war, most have forgotten about the mines, or just don't know."

Now I down my whiskey. This info is not very promising to me. I am stuck here, and I don't want to risk my body and life to clear the mines. No, no, there must be another way, damn it.

"I can see, you don't believe me, but you can drive thirty miles further and ask for Thomas. Bumbum Thomas they call him, and he made his name by clearing mines! He is a bit crazy and deaf now, but actually a very good guy. He can tell you more, if he is still alive. I don't know, haven't seen him for years," and he moves over his empty glass again. I fill it up, together with mine.

"One for the road," I add, while I pour.

I remember even Trevor in Dare es Salam mentioned a BumBum Thomas, but I didn't have a contact number or address, and the other numbers he gave me aren't working. Nevertheless, I need to find Bumbum Thomas.

I swop a box of cigarillos for two bottles of Scotch, and thank Mac for the nice talk. It seems he is happy too with the deal.

It is nearly evening, and I've had too much whiskey, and I have to take the chance with the only hotel in Tete where I can keep the car inside. I need a shower and food, and a good night's sleep. I'll look for Bumbum Thomas tomorrow. He is my last hope here.

I check in. It's totally overpriced, but there is hardly any accommodation available in this shitty town. Tourists won't stop here, and it doesn't look like any industry is picking up here either; only the horizontal, it seems, taking care of all the truck drivers.

The hotel even promises water 24/7. That must be the reason for the four stars they've painted behind the Hotel's name. Unfortunately, warm water is too much to ask for, but at least I get the dust off, and it wakes me up a bit. Then I make my way to the so-called hotel bar, and have some Coke to wake up further.

The menu looks good, but as soon I start smiling, the waiter points out what they don't have, so I ask him what they do have. Well, chicken... chicken... or chicken and chips. How I love Mozambique.

While I have a few beers and wait for my chicken, the story is caught in my brain, with endless thoughts crossing my head. I won't call them worries. Here I am in Mozambique, looking for old mines to build a cannon or a smart bomb into a boat, to deliver a unique message to the President of the United States; to get the world's attention.

Every time I've been in Mozambique it's been crazy. The first time was a visa break with more or less empty pockets. Then I took on the job in a backpacker to get over South Africa's winter. Then I went with a funny old lady to Ibo Island, to check the property market there, and now I want to get TNT, one and a half tonnes of it. From having this crazy idea to build a bomb, I am now at a point where it needs to become a reality. The prospects, however, are not too promising anymore. What if Bumbum Thomas is just another crazy person, stuck in poverty in this broken down country?

What then? Then would it have to happen only in my book?

And what about the promise to Brad's people?

That wouldn't be the real thing, and Brad wouldn't like it. It was his input that made me finally do all this, while I could be back in Cape Town, starting another little business. My phone rings. A voice screams, "STOP worrying!" Damn, I almost piss in my pants. That's Brad. He can read my mind even over hundreds of miles.

"Oh German, I know you are having supper somewhere and your brain is cooking. Stop it! Get yourself a girl, and relax. It will all be fine."

"Thanks, my friend, I know. I just feel a bit stuck."

"Well, haven't you been there before? But you always followed the little light at the end of the tunnel!?"

Yes, he is right, and I will find a solution for this problem too.

"How is it going with the boat?" I ask.

"It is fine. We worked hard all day, cleaned it up. We're ready for new construction when you back. And Clifford was a good help. Now he likes to introduce me to his sister."

"STOP it!" This time I am shouting at him. "Please don't play around in Beira. The girls are like mosquitoes: they all carry a virus. Don't do anything I wouldn't do. I will be back tomorrow!"

Then my chicken arrives, and I really enjoy it. I don't enjoy the old worn out mattress in my filthy room, but the experiences and worries of the day, and the alcohol, put me to sleep.

Early in the morning, the traffic wakes me. This rubbish hotel is in the middle of town, on a busy four-way crossing. I hate the noise, but I have to get up anyway. I'm not a morning person at all, and I am grumpy already, loaded with the problem I have to solve today.

Downstairs, I have to bribe the waiter to put the triple amount of coffee in my cup. It helps. The car is also still there, and washed and shining, and I do not mind tipping the poor street child who washed it. It's not like in Cape Town, where one guy will help you to park, one says he'll guards the car, and a third feels responsible for supporting you by guiding you out of the parking bay with wild signs executed with both hands. Not one of them gets the idea to clean the car in-between, but they all keep their hands open.

I drive further north looking for Bumbum Thomas. I've no address, no number, just his funny name. But I will do my best. Let's see where it takes me.

While I drive, I feel sorry for this land. The other Portuguese colony is getting rich through oil and diamonds. Angola is cooking. The Americans and Chinese are competing to see who gets the most oil out from there. Now that more or less every

Chinese is trading in his bicycle for a car, China needs more oil than the United States. I wonder how long the last oil resources will last.

I strongly believe that the Chinese, by using mainly bicycles, were a few step ahead if us. Well, at least they might have the smaller problem getting used to it again in a few years time!

Mac had said that there will be a T-junction, and I have to take a dirt road to the left for another five miles. Then I should come to a quiet, left-alone village, where I should ask for Thomas.

I believe I am on the right track, and keep on driving. Eventually, I see a bunch of houses, or what were once houses. There are no roofs, no windows and no doors. There are plenty of street dogs and, oh, there is someone cooking on a fire. Gosh it looks like one day after the war. I park the car in the middle of the village. Now there is some movement. People come and look at me, wondering what a man with a beautifully clean car wants here.

"*Senor* Thomas *por favor?*" I try with my bad Spanish, but there's no reaction. So I keep on walking, and I see only old women and children. The men must be somewhere at work. At the end of the road I see a cute-looking house. It's got a big cross painted on the one wall, and a little wooden tower with a rusty bucket as a bell. This must be the church here. Impressive. There is really no shop, nothing here in this forgotten place, but here's a little church, even well looked after. The door is open and I walk in. It smells like the few other churches I have been into in my life.

Benches are made out of all kinds of materials. Statues are well in order, and the atmosphere calms me down. I even sit down, and wonder what the universe is trying to tell me. Since I'm here, I put in some thoughts for my dead mother. What would she think about what I am going to do? Well, she would say I must know what I am doing, I'm old enough. Just so long as I have fun and am good and take care; true.

After quite a while in the church I walk out through a little door at the side and come into a graveyard; a huge graveyard it seems, as I turn my head. There must be hundreds, if not thousands, of graves. But why here? It is a bit scary and I turn around to leave, and nearly run over an old man. I am afraid, but he isn't. He just looks at me, and I at him.

What a funny creature he is. Under his priest dress, which is much mended, patch to patch, I can see a wooden leg. His face looks like it has been burned, and one eye is closed; the other one looks yellowish to me. A huge beard covers the rest of his face, so I can't make out if he is giving me a friendly or cross look. I apologize that I'd nearly run him over, and put my hand on his shoulder. Now he looks at me, and his yellow eye seems as if it is laughing at me.

I introduce myself. "I am William from South Africa. I was just driving around and..."

"... *auf der Suche nach mir*," he ends my sentence in German. What ghost is this now?

He answers in a funny German dialect, that I must have been on a search for him, and from my few English words he must have picked up my German accent. That's impressive, although it has happened a few times to me here in Mozambique, where a lot of people were educated in the former eastern Germany, through the socialistic regime.

"Surprised?" he mumbles in German into his beard.

"Yes," I answer in German.

"I am German-born and so are you. I am Thomas, or Bumbum Thomas," he tells me. "How come you are looking for me?"

I tell him about Mac, whom he doesn't know at all. Then I tell him why I was looking for him. He listens to me and then he offers me some tea. I take him up on his offer and follow him to a little hut, where he calls an older lady to make tea, and we sit down.

He gives me permanent goose pimples.

He looks at me and shakes his head. "Enjoy this tea. It's given to you by God. Enjoy this tea, and then go home. There is no work for you clearing mines. You are much too late. You will not find anyone to help you!"

"But if it gets paid nicely?" I ask.

He keeps on shaking his head, and repeats himself. "There is no one left who would help you."

"Oh, come on. Everybody needs work here, and would be thankful to find paid work. I can educate them!"

"You don't understand, my boy," he says slowly, and his yellow eye opens wide. "All the men who were once prepared to help, have done their job already!"

"But where are they?"

"Look around, can't you see them?" and he gestures with his arm over the graveyard. Now I get it, but can't even turn my head. Tears are pouring out of my eyes. How damn stupid have I been?

He says, "I can keep on crying, but it doesn't help anymore. They all met their death by clearing mines – one thousand and twenty three men of all ages. Some earned well for years, some only for days, but sooner or later, it got them all. Look at me! One leg missing, my face burned too many times to count. I lost one eye and a ear…" and I see that on his right hand only the two smallest finger are left. Scary. Very, very scary. I wish Brad were here with me.

I am speechless. I see all kinds of scenes passing though my mind, about the endlessly high number of horrible accidents which must have happened here. This graveyard will stop any man from trying to clear mines here. I guess that the story of each victim is known by every local, and how they will laugh about me when they get told why I came here. Bumbum Thomas keeps on telling me stories. He tells how primitively they tried to clear the mine fields, digging with bamboo in the ground, but not knowing all dirty tricks that can be played with mines. Personnel mines were at every little path, underground, or built in, to react through wires, deadly traps on nearly each square metre. Some were even connected with cables, so if one goes bang!, hundreds join the explosion and an entire field of hundreds of square metres goes up in dust.

It was worse than during the war, because then the locals just ran away. It was when the war was over, and they came back, that they died like flies. And nobody shows any responsibility for that, even though there are still hundreds of thousands of mines left underground and, any second, one could explode. That is why you don't see young people or men here. They left a long time ago. Only old women who've lost all their sons and husbands stay here and look after the graves.

I am speechless as he talks. Nobody had ever told me about this place, and the horrible events that had happened here. I guess that the Vietnam war was more important in those days, filling the media and papers because of the powerful America being involved, and the Mozambican civil war here never really reached the first world. The families of these victims never got any compensation. They wouldn't even know what that is.

Still he keeps on talking. "We have cleared tens of thousands of mines, and it still won't come to an end. People became more and more scared, till nobody wanted the dirty money for doing this deadly job."

"I understand," I throw in, and my tears come back. Why exactly I don't know. Probably because I feel sorry for all these poor people who got used so... and because I feel I've reached the end of my story and of my book.

And still he keeps talking. "When the time came that the authorities stopped sending soldiers to drive the mines away, and when they stopped paying the cheap labour, the men left. All that remained were thousand of mines!"

"Mines left? Where are they?"

"Look around, my boy," Thomas says. "What do you think I used to build the church? And the wall around the graveyard? Look at what you are sitting on!"

Now I freeze, and my heart pumps even harder. I am sitting on mines? I look down between my legs. Really! There I can make out four mines, sticking together above each other with a piece of wood in the middle.

"You don't have to be scared, my boy, there are no detonators left here, nothing will explode here, this is just pure, pressed TNT. No fire, no shot can detonate them. They are as dead as everything around you."

My tears stop, and my brain starts thrumming. So, everything here is built out of mines? My Lord! I've seen houses made out of old tyres, out of beer cans, out of plastic containers and cartons in Africa, but out of mines? That's unbelievable! Absolutely. What hot seat am I on here?

"Nobody will ever believe me about this"

"Yes, you are right," he confirms, "nobody will, but nobody makes the effort to get here and see. You are the first tourist in the last five years."

Gosh, will something like this repeat itself in Afghanistan, I wonder? There are also huge minefields there, to close up particular areas.

"Look," I put my hand back on his bony shoulder. "I am moved deeply, Thomas. I came here with some kind of childish idea, burned in by watching crazy movies. But this here is reality, and cannot stay hidden from the outside world.

"I will help to make it public, not only in the book I am writing. I will make sure that the press gets hold of this. You might get a few visits from journalists. If you do, please tell them just what you've told me. This is just too unbelievable."

He takes me by the hand, and we start walking around the graveyard wall. He explains how he built all this with his own bare hands. First he chopped the mines into brick-sized pieces, later he just used them as they were, and nobody in this region really cared what he did. Nobody comes here; too much fear. And nobody can help him, and he wants to build a proper tower for his church, and he points to an old water reservoir which is full of building material, full of mines – enough for a church tower, and enough for many other things. There are thousands of mines, dropped there like any other rubbish.

Okay, now I am quite awake. I grab his hand, and promise to help him to build the church tower, whatever it takes, and costs. His yellow eye starts smiling.

"You really will?"

"Yes, I will. I'll come back in a few days, and bring some friends and some tools. It is my pleasure to help."

Now his eye starts losing tears. "You make me happy, young man. God must have sent you to me. Well, don't over do it, but the universe is involved. I believe that so far."

I check my watch. I can still make it back to Beira in daylight. I give him a big hug, and promise to be back in three days at the most. Driving out of his ghost town, I am still shaking my head. There's been too much story, too much emotion in the last two hours. It's unbelievable, but there have also been good results for the mission.

I won't have to clear dangerous mines, no! No, things have come out very differently from how I had envisaged. I am going to build a church tower out of mines. No doubt, I will do that with Brad.

But I still have to find a way to get ownership of a few hundred of these mines. They are ready to pick up, but what will I tell Thomas? I grab a bottle of Scotch and a cigarillo from the back seat. I know that while I drive I can think best, and I want to have a plan before I reach Beira.

Three hundred mines are quite heavy. I would have to load the Landy a few times, and I'd have to camouflage them somehow. There are too many to crazy-bribe, hungry policemen on this road, and I do not want to be stopped and be seen with a load of pressed TNT, even though I wonder if these new young policemen would know what it is.

Nevertheless, I cannot take the risk. I will put them in old oil drums – yes, these drums have a thousand uses – and I will bring them to Thomas for my drinking water supply. Hmmm, that could work... Damn this Scotch and cigarillo are good. Lovely.

What a day it has been. I recall every word Thomas told me. I need to tell Brad the details, and that even as a Moslem he will have to help me to build a church tower. He promised me he'd do anything I tell him to; I got his word.

On the last five miles I buy a few kilo's of lobster from the street kids. One just has to check their eyes to see how fresh they are, and if they are still alive one can eat them. Boil them first for a minute to kill them and then grill them another minute on a barbecue. I mean the lobster, ...not the street kids!

BOAT AND TOWER BUILDING

Back at the farm, I see Brad and Clifford at the fire. Funny, they sit there, as I sat with... yes, with Harun a few months ago. But now Harun, I mean Brad, is telling the stories, and Clifford is trying to follow with his bad English. This picture makes me smile. How lovely. Brad is talking and talking. I clap his shoulder and ask how far his book is? Now it is about more than how to guard goats and sheep in the desert, isn't it? And he blasts out laughing.

"Yes, my best friend," he says, "much more, so much more. Life is amazing!" High five.

I tell him I have good news, and try to make my long story short. Up front, I tell him that my mission was successful, but it has got a price, which is a pleasure for me, and that he has to help me build a church tower!

"Yes, but..."

"Oh, no... no but!"

"Ok, we will."

I knew.

I boil the lobster for a minute, and then I cut them in half, pull out the grey *derms*, and brush them with garlic butter, before I put them on the barbecue.

Since Bangkok, Brad has been a fan of seafood, but it seems Clifford hates lobsters, even though he grew up with them, so I get some sausage for our other worker. I will not take him to the ghost town; nobody else needs to know what we do there,

Later, yes, I will make this forgotten issue known, but not now, while we will be driving around with mines in our car. So far we are really moving forward, even though earlier this day I have had a phase of strong doubts. But it really seems that the universe wants us to accomplish our mission. Now I know, I am sure: we will deliver the message!

The supper is a feast, and I am happy about how the boat looks, although there is quite some work to do, which reminds me of the time when I built up my Borgward, which was built in 1952, also burnt out, and I made a fun car out of it. And fun we will have again here too, I love working and building with my hands, and bringing my creativity into perspective. What a lovely job to do, under Africa's sun, and a great beach further down. Now it all seems to be falling into place.

There is just something missing here. "Hey Clifford, what is this about your sister?"

"Oh, my sister. She is still working now late shift..."

Hmmm, shit I thought so!

"Yes, she is a nurse in the hospital here."

A nurse, so she is a decent girl, I think to myself. And where there is one nurse, there must be more, and I catch Brad's smile.

"Clifford, why don't you invite her here with her friends? Then we make a big barbecue?"

Now he smiles too. "Yes, we can do that. This weekend she is off."

"That's fine, let's make a plan. Tomorrow I need to organize some oil drums. I might ask Richard where to get them, or, Clifford, do you know where we can buy a few oil drums?"

"Yes, I know, down at the refinery. We need to ask the workers there." He will do that for us. That is good. Then I will get some tools for us, some saws and long, strong nails, which we'll need for the tower. And maybe we'll go back there tomorrow already, together with lots of food supply for Thomas and us, and for the village people. It shouldn't take longer than two days to build the tower in this scary ghost town. I still get goose pimples when I think about his past.

From this night we stay in the farm house. The old lady fixed up some rooms for us, and we make ourselves at home. I always have to hide the bunch of cash dollar notes, and the highly sensitive capsules from Trevor, this time in the cistern of the toilet. Before I fall asleep at the fire, I hit the sack, and fall asleep very happily. The sea breeze still hits us out here. Lovely.

By the time I get up for coffee, Clifford has already brought us the results for the oil drums. We can have as many as we want, and they are eight dollars each. They might be stolen, but we are no choosers – we need them. I will let them boil out with saltwater, and get them painted, and cut the lid open to put the mines in. I still need to find a story to tell Thomas about what we are going to use them for. The question will come, no doubt.

Richard has recommended to me a useful hardware store, where I get tools, nails and two saws. And I even spot some fibreglass paste there, quite expensive, but we do need that stuff to fix up the boat. With my second morning coffee I spend some time to get an idea of how to build the boxes for the mines. They will be fully built in. Nobody will ever get to see them when in the boat. In the remaining space I will build in containers for drink water and petrol for the engine. And much more we won't take on board; just food and us.

Damn sure, we will be overweight already, but there's nothing we can do about that. We are not joining a race. We just need to get safely to America, slowly but surely. I'm really looking forward to the day we start our sailing journey from here.

While I drive with Clifford to get the oil drums, he points out his sister to me on the sidewalk. Oh, my Lord, that's just my cup of tea. Booked! I'm sure that one of her friends will be suitable for Brad, to help him get over his heart pain about Jessica, his first real love after a few short affairs in Bangkok.

In the evening we get all ready to leave next day to visit Thomas, and the next day we set off. We leave Clifford behind, guarding our boat, with some sanding jobs to do.

I enjoy long talks with Brad during the drive. It's much better when there's nobody to hear what we are talking about. I explain to him in detail how the landmines work, and that there is no threat or danger while we sail, because the capsules are outside the load. He has to trust me anyway. I also mention that, back home where he was a shepherd, there are plenty of minefields too, which might be better registered these days on a computer and a military data base, but if a real war hits the fan, all this admin stuff sometimes disappears, or gets destroyed, and then Afghanistan could end up with the same hassle as here.

What I am talking about he fully understands when I show him the big graveyard, shortly after our arrival, before Thomas appears out of nowhere like a ghost.

I introduce Brad, and we have some tea, while I pass some of our groceries – plenty of chicken and vegetable, rice and pasta – on to his old lady. Food is important when I work hard. I show Thomas some hand drawings which I've done, and let him choose what kind of tower he wants. He picks one of the four ideas, and he is very happy with what will be built.

We use the Landy like a tractor, picking the mines out of the water reservoir, and driving them up the hill – over more mines – straight to the construction place.

It is a nice building. We hit nails through the mines as if they were big, round Gouda cheeses. In the end, we will plaster them nicely with clay from the ground, as Thomas has already done with the wall and the chapel.

While driving up the hill, Brad fills two drums with mines for us. Yes, we more or less steal them, but I cannot see any harm in doing this. We take only what we need, and my last bad conscience I will satisfy by donating a new and much bigger bell for the tower. So what, let's call it recycling.

The construction goes fast. It's nearly like building with my beloved old Lego in my childhood. At four metres high, where our self-made bamboo ladder comes to an end, I build the contrivance for the bell, for which I bought some wooden pillars in Chimoio. From there we finished off the tower with a further two metres, a peak and a big iron cross on top, which I'd already welded in Beira for that purpose.

By this time we also have four drums full of mines in our car. It's not enough, but it's a good start. We will have to come back with the bell anyway.

Thomas is proud and happy. He hugs us endlessly, and calls the village people, and gives out the food we'd brought with us. Brad and I are happy to. I enjoyed how I worked, hand-in-hand with him. It all worked out easily and nicely.

The locals love us, and are touched by the help we've given. Brad and I feel good.

Next morning, after coffee and tea, we shoot back to Beira, where we hide the mines in a hidden space I've found in the barn. After filling the hole, we park our boat on them. It should be safe. I do not want to be questioned by anyone about what we need the mines for, although I should actually think about an explanation for if the situation arises.

We need to be prepared for everything. I hope that the farmer is not coming back earlier than we've been told.

Then we go straight back via Chimoio, where a friend has organized me a big bell. I don't ask where it's from, and pay forty dollars for it.

Thomas is happy when he sees his new bell, and can't stop saying thank you. I get the idea to plaster the front of the church nicely, to build a kind of nice entrance. Thomas appreciates the idea.

"Oh, do whatever you want to do. It is so nice what you build already."

Okay, great. We drive down and load more mines, four drums for us, and hundreds for the outside area.

But this is still not enough. One drum takes thirty mines and I need at least two more drums. Well, we will just visit him in a week's time again, when we've got further with the boat. We know that there is lots of supply available, and we know he will always be happy to see us.

The outside area is quickly laid, and now it looks clean and proper. I feel good. I really have done something good here, and in exchange my biggest headache, how to get the mines, got solved to.

Next day, we are back in Beira. We have a cellar full of mines, a boat that needs to be fixed, it's thirty-two degrees, there's cold beer, and hopefully lots of gorgeous nurses waiting for us. Lovely.

I send an email to uncle Achmeth:

"I'm glad I have everything I need for the party, will be a blast!"

He answers:

"Good to hear. I have a lovely present ready for you, that will make you happy forever!!"

I sleep so well these days. I am just happy with how everything is going forward, with no trouble... touch wood. Sometimes I feel like Noah, when he was building his ark, and everybody thought he was crazy... until he finally succeeded.

I decide that we will work hard from Monday till Friday, and have fun over the weekends. Fair enough. So, every weekend I try to spend lots of time sailing with different dhows and boats, picking up the sailors' techniques and skills. It is fascinating, to catch the wind, and speed up. These dhows are made out of massive pieces of solid wood, and weigh a few times what our trimaran weighs, so if we are a bit overloaded I don't think that it will be a problem. My plan is to always stay as close to the coast as possible. The speed of travel is not important, and I live in the hope that the transatlantic sail will go as smoothly as it did twenty years ago.

On the first Saturday we prepare for the barbecue with fish and meat, and lots of drinks, Clifford's sister will join us with some nurses. It's time that I get a health check up, what with my lifestyle.

And here they come... My goodness, the dress code here is not comparable with Cape Town, but a few of them are really gorgeous, and speak a few words of English. It reminds me of Thailand: with twenty words one can really get what one wants, but still don't need to have long, boring conversations!

So, to make a long story short, we once again get what we urgently need for relaxation during these hard weeks of hard labour here.

Life goes on like this. We work hard, live hard, and nobody tells me what I've got to do. I can sleep as long as I feel like, but here I don't get up too late since we have early nights.

I am so concentrated on the boat building that I sometimes forget what the whole purpose of it is. I'm glad that there is no institution checking what we build, having to go, such as my good old Borgward had to, through a road worthy test in Germany. The Borgward failed under all kinds of stupid old rules and laws. Here I am the law for the construction side.

It was quite a mission to get the adjustment of the engine right. Yes, I will put our lovely, strong five litre V8 Mercedes engine in here, so if all sailing skills fail we can do plenty of miles by engine. One of the oil drums I use as a tank. I just have to use a bit pipe for the cooling system, and get the gear shaft for the automatic gearbox in place. It is hard work, but no problem.

The biggest job is to get the shelves right for the TNT load. We have to cut most of the mines into shape to make them fit. All the cut-off waste we use to fill the gaps in-between.

The heavy weight of the TNT load will be at the back of the boat, the engine more or less in the middle, and we will have to use the front for groceries, and for water tanks, which we can adjust to balance the weight in the back.

The concept of our cannon is based on that of a "hollow load", which one would have used to blow up bridges in Germany, with smaller "cutting " loads, which one would have lined up on a particular course to cut metre-thick concrete! All important highway bridges in Germany were made ready to be blown up in case the cold war turned into a hot war! Then Germany would have cut all main connections from the east by blasting parts of highways and bridges, being careful to do minimum damage so that it could all be quickly built up again, after the possible war was over.

So my calculation for our "cannon" is that the TNT load is attached to the boat's end in a half circle, a particular V-angle, around the big engine. A strong, powerful detonation will melt the engine in less than a second, and shoot it forwards like a huge bullet, which will be seen as a huge, hot fireball. At the same time, the fibreglass body and the rest of the boat will melt and burn away.

Powered by one and a half tonnes of TNT, the bullet will have enormous thrust, and should be able to hit through anything closer than four hundred metres away!

The only difficulty is to get Walky in the right position, and to get the timing right for the cannon shot. I need to work on that.

With the same system, just using much smaller loads – not even fifty grams – one shot petrol stores in Vietnam through the fence, from the outside. By using a hanging plate, a coin glued in the middle, and a round layer of TNT at the plate's border, this brought the coin to a melted hot bullet, which could blow up petrol barrels fifty metres away.

Unfortunately, I can't do any exact calculations, but with the old formula still in my mind I feel sure that this cannon will work. I am not finished yet, but the concept is in place.

From one of the other boat owners I get an old navigation system. He says it is already three years old... bloody useless. He makes me laugh. He is one of the victims of today's electronic economy. He most probably buys a new laptop every year, and a new cell phone every six months. Oh well, if it makes him happy.

So I wonder what he would say to the navigation system we had in 1991, when I crossed the Atlantic. This "stone age" system got us exactly where we wanted to be, and even I could work it out. I hate all these new electronic, time-wasting gimmicks. For example, all I need from a cell phone is for it to be just a phone. I don't want to watch movies, or use it as a magic mixer or hair drier... just a phone, please.

For the sail I've approached a local old fisherman. He's actually a guy who fixes the sails for the dhows here. He will make us a sail for quite a reasonable cost, in the size I've told him.

Ropes and winches I even got here in Beira, surprise, surprise!

And what is good for a wooden dhow is good for us. We keep it simple, one of my oldest rules.

Each evening, while I have my sundowner beer, I can look back at what we have archived so far. If we keep on going forward at this speed, we will launch the boat into the sea in two weeks' time. By then the farmer will be back and I'd hate observing eyes while we build our romantic navy shuttle.

There must be a bit of luxury, and we build in a mega loudspeaker system, the same as all the local mini taxis have. I do need the inspiration of music, and we will be at sea for quite a long time. During that time I will get this crazy story on paper – well, into my laptop. I'm wondering already, what will the happy ending be?

For this weekend I was planning a short trip to Zimbabwe to renew our Mozambican visas, and a visit to Thomas, but on the other hand, if we leave here one afternoon, do we need an exit stamp in our passport? Any additional border post comes with some danger. I will put in some more thought on that issue, but I send Clifford to find out if we can get another visa here in Beira.

Brad and I hardly speak about our mission. We just do what we need to do. There are no more worries coming up, since now it is all up to us. The short emails between Uncle Achmeth and me tell me that they are with us, and that they are expecting our mission to work out as they wish. In a few months, it will be ten years since the World Trade Centre in New York got hit on September eleven. I've never forgotten that day. The TV documentation didn't stop, and the world really did stop breathing. Something totally unexpected happened to America, and there was a high number of innocent victims. But I wonder about the story behind it: how many years was it planned for? And did the parties involved ever expect another crazy war as a result, a war that's already taken nearly ten years, without any other achievements than horrendous costs and innocent casualties. Who is going to end this war?

Well, how would it be if the country that started the whole shit got a wakeup call with our-eye opening message, which will not cost a drop of blood, and not even a cent of taxpayers' money. Lovely!

We get another month's Mozambican visa without any problems, just a little additional bribing fee, and we have it the same day that we applied.

On Sunday we go to church – to our church tower.

Thomas is very happy to see us. We bring more groceries, and greet the locals. Their spirit has changed already. Thomas must have told them what we're going to do. We have made this TNT Chapel, a new tourist attraction, and will create further business and attention for the locals, and their story.

Since we parked our Landy down there in the shade, we quickly fill up our two drums with more mines, while the locals enjoy the great Sunday feast that we brought.

In the evening we go with our nurse fan club to our beloved pub at the sea, while watching the fishermen coming in with their dhows. It's somehow majestic, how these old ships cruise the sea.

By end of the following week, I want all containers and shelves to be ready to be loaded with TNT. I've done some extra preparations in Walky for our safety too; one never knows what danger might hit us out on sea. There are thieves and crazy pirates out on the sea up north, and we do not have any weapons to defend ourselves with, so I've had to do a different kind of preparation to Walky, in case the shit hits the fan.

Getting the engine in will be the very last step, since we still need the car daily. To do that, I'm well prepared. I've got a heavy, strong iron frame, which will also be a support for the bullet-to-be. When the time is right, I can add some left-over mines to multiply the power of a possible hit; that is if we are ever going to use what we've built here.

The coming weekend will be our last here in Beira. As it always is with happy days, I wonder where the time has gone. We start stocking groceries; nothing fancy, mostly dried fruit, biscuits, and lots of biltong from a Zimfarmer. There's no space for beer, so Scotch must do. And yes, of course, three hundred litres of water in fifteen containers, all well fixed in the bow, so that we can use their weight to change the balance of the boat, if need be.

Added to the car battery, we've got a 220 volt converter, that we can use to charge our cell phones and laptop, and Brad's beloved iPad, which he still treats like the biggest treasure in his life. Well, where would he be without this invention? Could we maybe later blame Microsoft or Apple for what we are doing? No, I don't think so.

On Friday we have a big party and invite the farmer and all the friends we have made, and our nurses, who are as sad as Clifford, but he might be taken over by the farmer as a little helper. And of course there are mixed feelings coming up, although fewer worries. The next phase will start an exciting sailing journey around southern Africa. Lovely.

I send Uncle Achmeth a short mail:

"I am so happy. Our voyager trip starts soon, and we are pretty loaded"

He answers shortly after:

"We are looking forward to an unforgettable welcome with fireworks!"

On Saturday morning I take the engine out of our Landy. I am a bit sad; I loved that car. It did a real good job.

With a steel construction and our own winch we manage to lift the engine from the car into the boat, where the frame and all kinds of pipes and cables are waiting to be connected. We're not as fast as in formula one, but very good German preparation worked out fantastically. After an hour, all is connected as it has to be, and I can even start the engine. It takes up work, as always before in the Land Rover chassis. Richard will come later to take us with his trailer to the beach, where I will christen the boat once again:

"WALK THE TALK!"

Richard will sell the Landy for us. It is a bit different without an engine, but luckily we are not depending on the sale. We tell him, whenever he sells it, to give half to Thomas, and half to Clifford.

Now it is the moment where Walky will slip into the sea. I can't wait to see how deep it will sit in the water. I made some calculation using a little paper boat that I folded, and filled with sand accordingly. I guess that's the way that the old Egyptians did it too. My paper boat swam fantastically, and was perfect by the measurement in the water depth, although it went down after a minute, because it sucked up water. Walky won't do that.

Walky slips into the bluish sea. There are lots of spectators around, mostly wanting to see how it speeds with the heavy engine. So do I. But first I christen it with a bottle of champagne, and thankfully it dances nicely, not to deep in the water. I am happy. We did a damn good job. Brad is impressed, although as it slips into the water he realizes what a little home it will be for us for the next few weeks.

My thoughts about where home will be after the boat, I keep to myself. There is still a long way to go.

We picked up our exit stamp from the immigration office on Friday and we fill up the drink water at the jetty. Then we do a little drive, just a few miles up and down the coastline with the engine and the whole nurse crowd and Clifford, to see how Walky will behave. So far I am impressed, although, if the sea gets rough, it will be a different story.

We set the sail, while we have another experienced sailor on board. I am speechless over what we have achieved here, and it will make me sad, if I have to make the call, to bring the cannon into use.

We test the boat for a few hours, making all kinds changes to the sail, so that Brad and myself know how to move on the boat, and what to focus on. One of us will always be awake, while the other one will sleep.

All goes even better than expected, and we end the test with a lovely sundowner cruise. Then we anchor Walky close to the beach, where Clifford has got our fish barbecue waiting. It becomes a long night, with even a few tears from the girls, but that's part of a traveller's life. Long after midnight we sneak into Walky and enjoy a peaceful sleep, waking up early with the sun, and dipping straight into the sea for a wake up swim. Lovely.

It's time to get used to saltwater showers, because the stored water is only for drinking and cooking.

AROUND AFRICA'S COAST

We lift the anchor, pull up the sail and start sailing south. Clifford and the girls came back to wave us bye-bye. I'd tried to get around that scenario – I like warm welcomes, but not warm bye-byes and farewells. Here the city passes away, with a last look at the miserable Grand Hotel, and after half an hour the shabby "skyline" of Beira is gone.

On we go. Soft music is playing, and I feel like flying. There is no motor noise, just sea and wind... what a dream. We will pass the beautiful island Bazaruto in front of Vilanculos, and we will even pass Torfu beach, close to Inhambawne, beautiful party places I know from the past. But since we are riding a cannon ball, nearly as old Munchausen did in his saga, I do not want to make any unnecessary stops, even though it will be tempting sometimes. It would be too dangerous.

I start writing my book. It is so alive in me, and I can't believe that it is not even two months since we left Afghanistan. I didn't give a lot attention to the news, but I know the shit is still on, with some "wanna-be politician" making wild promises about when to leave there, and about when Afghanistan might be ready to look after itself again. James-Bond-style-dressed, our German minister of defence plays hard, looking good on TV, visiting the troops in the war zone.

But what does that guy know about army and war? He fucked up as Minister for Economy, and then became Minister of Defence. It makes me laugh. What job swopping is that? In a country like Germany, where you have to have a three-year apprenticeship to sell bread, and then you won't be allowed to sell meat because for that you need to study again, but you can go from one ministerial post to the other in a few days! Poor politics. For me a defence minister should be only an old, experienced general, not a spoilt playboy. But they just talk for the press and media, and before any new election. Time wasters!

They've lost the relation to reality. They can't even hit vehicles without killing the breeding animals around the target, so how do you pick who are the good ones and who are the bad ones in this warzone? They would do better to keep their eyes open in their own country.

We learn later that some excitement comes up in the head office of the Americans in Kabul. The brother of the dead soldier, the one from whom Brad got his iPad, is complaining that the bank accounts got cleaned up with various credit cards in Bangkok, and he wants an explanation from his brother's superior. They dig in their files and find the date and place where his dead body was found after a tricky ambush. From there, the corpse followed the normal procedure, and was sent home to the States. So how can his cards be used in Thailand, he wants to know? Well, the officers there, who are already stressed out from the situation and the circumstances they live in, don't have time to pay any attention to forgotten dead people's private stuff.

An officer tells the story later, like a joke in the canteen, where he caught the attention of one journalist – one of the useless and success-less catastrophe journalists, named Harry – to whom this sounds like a story. Well, at least the start of one.

Harry works himself to the contact details of the brother of the dead soldier. He gets curious and wants to follow up what could have happened, especially since he spends his off time mostly in Bangkok, as one of the sex tourists, where he is one of the stupid victims who believe the bar girls there when they say they love you!

He makes some notes about what he will investigate, when there the next time.

In the next week he is approached by another soldier, who found the dead soldiers dog tags in a campfire, close to a miscalculated airwave used to fight back a hijacked convoy. The identification tags only got found because they'd had to burn nearly a hundred goats and sheep, which had been hit by mistake, in the same fire. These were Harun's animals.

On a map he makes out the distance between the spot where the soldier was found, and where the fire is. This doesn't make sense to him, till another soldier watching over his shoulder, shakes his head. This soldier knows the campfire place. On being asked about it he says, "Best you ask the German who runs the kitchen outside of town, where they are rebuilding the highway! That German guy is his friend and spends mostly every evening there!"

Out at sea, the days are very peaceful. The sea is quiet and there are no clouds. Brad and I are just resting, but I still do my daily workouts to stay fit, and we swim in the middle of the sea, just so long as one of us stays on board. Brad watches all sorts of downloaded movies, and I write my book.

The words just flow out of my writing hand, because now it is not fantasy, now it's an experience that I write down. The happy end only, I will have to leave with my fantasy, before I present the book to specialists in the movie industry in the States.

We're making an average of thirteen knots an hour, about twenty kilometres an hour. That's not a lot, but it's a comfy way of getting forward. It is like a walk in the park. We have lots of time; it is the fifteenth of July today.

Even here a routine sets in. Brad usually sleeps after supper and one or two whiskeys, and I sleep only after midnight, into the morning, with a few additional snoozes during the day in the sun, after workout and lunch.

After two days we pass the islands in front of Vilanculos. One needs a permit to go on land, and we just pass by. It is too busy here. There are too many South African holiday makers, and charter boats. I want to leave that area behind us, so we change our course a bit further out to sea, away from the hustle and bustle. Out there, the wind calms down, and the sea gets quite flat, so we take the chance to boil some spaghetti on our gas cooker, turn up our sound and have an early whiskey for a change. We really do try not to drink too much, but we are a bit bored, and the music entertains, and Brad's idea to take some nurses with us up until Maputo wasn't the worst idea he'd ever had... but we didn't.

Then I pick up a funny noise. A voice? Can that be?

I get out of the kitchen corner and spot another boat close by. What I see, cannot be true. It had better not be; this experience is not needed.

I look at a seven-foot black guy, with a machine gun and ammunition around his monstrous chest that covers his red shirt from Pizza King Nairobi. Brad shouts, "What's up?" and I ask him if he's ordered some pizza. Before he comes up to check on me, I feel a hard hit with the gun to my chin and drop flat on the boat, feeling pain in my teeth and with blood running out of my mouth. Now I am awake. Fucking pirates, so far south. What do they want from us?

Damn. This is worse than in a bad movie. I spot Brad standing frozen, hands high up in the air. At least he's learned something from his action movies. Then I get another kick from the pizza boy into my back. It is painful. He is pissing me off now. I haven't been in a bad mood for ages, but now I really feel shit, even though my favourite song from Bon Jovi is still playing loudly: "Its my life".

I see their boat. It must be a speedboat stolen from tourists. There are three more guys on it, all with guns to hand. I hear the big guy screaming, "Money, give me your money!" Sure, he knows from experience that every sailor has got his cash and paper cleverly hidden somewhere on his boat.

"Okay, okay," I stumble with my bleeding tongue, and give a sign that I want to get up and get it. With another kick he gets me doing so. I get up and tell him I need my keys. "Keys, keys," I repeat and point to the steering wheel, where the keys are in the ignition, and where my cell phone also lies. Do I have a little surprise ready for them! Since I also watch a few action movies, I've prepared something that even Brad doesn't know about. I've always believed in acting totally scared and nervous if something like this happens. I have been in similar situations in the Amazon, when they wanted to shoot me after they'd shot my tires and got the money. Luckily, they'd run out of ammunition and I only heard a click at my head. Yes, I've always been guarded by an army of guardian angels. This guy, however, has got at least two hundred shot around his neck, not counting what the others have.

The guy hits me again, and this lets me fall to my keys and against our steering wheel. The boat immediately turns ninety degrees, the big guy stumbles and I press quick-dial two on my cell phone. At the same second, Walky's right beam explodes in front and something hits the speed boat, which goes off in flames. At the same moment I give the pizza boy a push overboard, and start the V8 and give full power. "Its my life" is still coming loudly from the loudspeaker – it all happened very quickly – and in seconds we are half a mile behind the burning and sinking speedboat. One guy is swimming and screaming around in the sea, but sorry, we didn't order pizza!

Brad is still standing frozen. I shout at him a few times until he starts moving towards me. "It is all fine," I say, "all good. Get the whiskey bottle: I need a double one."

The left beam of Walky hangs there in half, like an old banana skin. We need to move our weight to the left beam. I shout at Brad to move at least eight water containers on the left beam to get a better balance. We won't go down, but it will be difficult to stay on course like that. we need somehow to fix it in, and for that we need to get on land, so I change course direction to the coast. At full speed, I guess that we make twenty-five knots now. Lovely.

After I down the whiskey, I hug Brad. He is shivering all over.

Too much happened in only a few minutes, and he still can't get what actually happened to us.

"What? What?" he screams, and looks at our right beam. I try to calm him down. Everything is fine. We were very, very lucky, and I am glad that I had built a tiny little shot into the right beam, just in case something like this happened. This shot was done with only ten kilo's of TNT, the material from two mines, with an old axe in the middle. Formed like a V, it shot straight forwards into the pirates' speedboat, and must have hit the petrol pipe or the tank. It had worked lovely!

The main cannon will work as well, just with more than a hundred times the load. And at that time we will not be on board because afterwards there won't be anything left of this boat.

We're coming closer to the beach. There are no buildings or people to see. This must be the endlessly long coconut plantation north of Xai Xai. The navigation system proves me right. Okay, I think we can take a chance. As the noise of a hundred goats screaming and eating under the trees welcomes us, Brad jumps off board with the rope and ties us to the first coconut tree. We feel safe. My heart is still pumping like a steam train, and my tongue and lip are bleeding like mad, but we are alive. This could have turned out quite badly, but we were lucky. That was real action now, and Bruce Willis couldn't have done it better!

Yes, I have heard about the pirate stories, but I hadn't imagined that they were so far south. I hope that there are not more of them. We don't have any other weapon.

We end up chopping some bamboo to rebuild the beam. It will look funny, but it will do the job: African art. We've nearly finished the bottle of whiskey since the attack, but we didn't kill anyone. What we did do was in self-defence, and I cannot see a court case for that coming up. Nevertheless, I still want to get as far away, as quickly as possible, as we can.

We load lots of coconuts. The idea to steal a goat I let go. It would only bring an innocent shepherd, like Brad had once been, into trouble. Two hours later, we speed with engine power out on sea, and I keep on speeding for another four hours at nearly the full power of the Mercedes engine.

I still feel itchy. We all know the feeling when something's happened to us, and we just want to get away as fast as possible. It all looks the same on the water and by sunset we slow down, switch off the engine, and sail ahead. Thanks be that God is with us; Allah too. And that the whole village around Thomas' church is praying for us daily.

Yes, this was an experience not needed, but I am impressed by my little cracker, which blew up the boat. The explosion from cookie one will be huge, if it is ever needed.

Brad is a bit pissed off that I hadn't told him, but I thought he would be too scared, since this cracker was sharp, and if anyone had mistakenly dialled the particular cell phone number that I'd connected to one of the electric capsules in the cracker, we might have had much more trouble!

When I explain this all to him, and the different of size of our main cracker, he starts smiling, and claps my shoulder. "William, whatever you do is great. I feel safe with you, and you saved my new life today!"

Then he lies down and sleeps, and I steer the boat and enjoy Africa's sky and stars. There is a warm wind. Things were really sharp today, but it is these kind of things that one has to live through in order to write it in a book.

The next days go easily. The wind changes a few times, but the sea is lovely. We should soon get into South African waters. Coming home. There we will visit an immigration office at the Marina in Richards Bay, enjoy some steaks, stock up with groceries and fuel, and maybe even find a better replacement for the bamboo beam, which always gets partly full of water.

Before that, however, we get hit by heavy rain, which turns into a storm. I put the sail on half mast; safety comes first. Brad gets seasick, and is throwing up all he ate in the last few days. I know how bad it is, but there is hardly any help. We've no medicine on board, but I don't trust medicine anyway – if you are seasick, then you are seasick – and I tell him to hang in there. Or to get up and look and focus somewhere on a fixed point on the horizon, and to ignore the wild sea around him. It seems that he calms down, while he holds himself tight to the mast, in addition to a rope that both of us have tied to the boat, in case we get thrown overboard.

It takes nearly all night, and only shortly before sunrise does it stop. Neither of us sleeps for a second, and we are totally exhausted. I tell him to lie down and sleep. It doesn't matter that everything is wet, he sleeps on the dot.

According to our navigation system we are past Ponto de Ouro, so are nearly in South African waters, safe from pirates, I hope. And I might have some good red wine very soon. Lovely.

The sea is already getting colder. It is winter in South Africa, so we should get something warmer for the next weeks. The same afternoon, we check in at Richards Bay. Luckily it is raining again, so there are no people around to ask stupid questions about what happened to our boat. If they do ask, then it was a shark attack, wasn't it?

We make it in the last minutes before the closing of the immigration office. There's no problem there at all. Then we go shopping for food and warm staff – and red wine to warm up – and get to sleep early. We both have to catch up on some sleep, and a whole night, more than ten hours, will just be fine after a bottle of red.

Next morning, the South African sun welcomes us and Brad realizes that I am actually at home, even if still two thousand miles from Cape Town, but yes, on home soil – or water. And we are sailing under the South African flag now. Lovely.

We will pass my home town in the next ten days, and by then I need to decide if we go transatlantic alone, or if I'm going to hire an experienced friend. But I think the decision was made a long time ago. I will not risk any one else's life on our mission and any other person spending any time on board would get suspicious about the funny construction, and the heavy weight at the back. So, we will go alone. We can do it.

And the bamboo-fixed beam makes us two freaks, at whom everybody would laugh. Nobody would ever imagine that these two freaks have got something totally different in mind. Let them laugh, like I let my friends laugh when I said I would write a book, and would get a movie made out of it, and finally earn some millions. Oh, how they laughed.

I can understand. I would have laughed too at someone. But this time I will laugh last.

We cruise along the South African coastline. I feel safe here, and know many of the towns we are passing. Hopefully, I'll drive along here with a nice 4x4 in a few months, on the lookout for a suitable small holding or farm for me, when dreams come true. Lovely.

I do know that there are thousands of shipwrecks around Cape Agulhas, the most southern tip of the African continent, and at Cape Point, the most south western tip, so I wait for the best weather conditions to sail around there. It is very exciting for me, since I've lived in this areas for nearly fifteen years, and now I really feel like one of the old pirates, with a basically equipped, primitive boat, and a huge cannon on board. All the way along this stretch of coast, I tell Brad my experiences there, and how fantastic the inland is, and promise to show him it all, at a later stage.

In Cape Town itself I don't feel like a stop. With my luck, in the first hour I'll meet a handful of people who know me.

I am too tense for long conversations and talks now. I am busy with my book, and I write most of the day. This book is the first priority; nothing else is as important at this time.

So, we pass the beautiful city of Cape Town. Brad is impressed by the landscape, with the massive table mountain, and the city's lovely beaches. Yes, it is most probably one of the most beautiful cities in the world, for me anyway, and it is home to me.

I decide to stop for a last big shop only up the west coast in Langebaan, about two hundred miles up north.

It is cold and wet these days, and kind of uncomfortable, with a few sweaters and a fleece jacket on top. How lovely it was in northern Mozambique, but I do know it will be hot again in about two weeks' time, in Brazil. I can't wait for the moment when we spot land on the other side of the Atlantic. I'll never forget how it was twenty years ago. I just jumped into the water in my shorts, and swam nearly half an hour to a little beach bar on the fascinating island of Fernando de Neronha. I couldn't walk straight. I tumbled and fell down in the sand, just not used to solid ground under my feet after two weeks' sailing, but I entered Brazil swimming. Lovely it was.

I make use of the Langebaan Lagoon to wait for better conditions, and I use these days to fix up our bamboo beam with more fibre paste and rope. And of course we fill up with water, petrol and groceries, including plenty of whiskey.

Before leaving, I send uncle Achmeth an email:

"Dear uncle, I might be broke after the party. Here are my bank details!"

And I give him my bank details in Thailand.

He replies:

"These parties are always expensive. Just so long as they are worth it! I'll help you back on your feet. The twin sister party ten years ago had a much higher price. Hope you will be in time!"

Goossshh, I thought about that all the time. This year it will be ten years after the crazy plane crash into the World Trade

Centre, and ten years of war for nothing, and what a kick and message it will be if we manage to accomplish our mission on the same date!

Damn, this will make people and politicians think. Nobody can ignore this, or keep his eyes closed then, and everybody who's got a bit of human brain left should think more than twice about what needs to be changed, and what has to stop after ten years of wasting lives and money by this US cowboy president.

No more proof needed!

TRANS ATLANTIC

On the morning of the 20th of July, we leave Langebaan and course north west. I prefer to be out at sea than in waters in front of Angola or Nigeria, knowing it will be at least two weeks – long weeks – before we touch ground again.

I bear in mind, that nobody actually knows where I am, and what I am doing, and why bother to tell them. I love to share success afterwards, but don't want to worry others beforehand.

It was the same twenty years ago. Nobody in my family knew I was sailing across the Atlantic. I saved them the sleepless nights, and only called once I had safely arrived in Brazil.

If I had got lost when I hitchhiked a few weeks later from Rio de Janeiro, right across the whole Amazon to Caracas in Venezuela, in a six-week torture, most probably nobody would have ever heard of me again. I believe I was lucky a lot of times, and today I worry even less and just live it. All men have to die once, but not all men have lived!

It this point I don't know that someone is worried. This damn American journalist Harry is in Bangkok and following up where the soldier's credit cards had been used. Back in Mazar he'd noticed that Harun and I had left at the same time, and found out that I had been seen on a bus to Pakistan. He's even got two credit card slips from the German beer garden in Bangkok, where we had the first feast, and has compared the signature on them with my food orders in the camp. There is no doubt that the long W that I always stretch on any documents is the same as the ones I signed on all the food orders in Mazar. Now he makes up the case, his case and story-to-be, and he is determined to bring people who steal from dead heroes to justice.

With the proof of my dumb signature, he gets the authorities' attention, and they do follow up and discover that I flew to Nairobi a while ago. Harry is more excited than we are. He's got his own case, for the first time in his life.

Since he'd already failed a few times to pass the assessment to join the police force, he is trying to make a living as a freelance journalist, as thousands do. That's why we get all these hero stories from war and conflict zones, which are ninety percent fantasy, and written in hotel rooms, because, at the end of the day, these camera heroes are always too late, or at the wrong time at the wrong spot. So how lucky is he, being alone on this case!

Oblivious of all this, I enjoy the peaceful sailing, Brad leaves me alone to write my book. Being very concentrated on my work, and given that there is not much to do other than keep my eyes open, the next days go quickly. There are a few weather changes, a few little storms, but nothing too rough, and we are well on our way: just joined by dolphins.

After fourteen days we are as high as Recife. I've got memories of this crazy city too… lovely ones. I use our engine as much as possible. I've no time for flat winds from wrong directions; this is no sailing competition or cruise, and this is the mission of my lifetime.

We had to stop close to Recife to fill up with water, fuel and groceries. I hate that big city coastline, with thousands of people trying their luck at fishing to get something eatable on their table, or in their hands. The Brazilians paddle on wooden boards amongst all kind of rubbish in the dirty, filthy, stinky coastline waters.

I would love to have another party holiday further north, on a dream beach in Fortaleza, which is very tempting, but now time is pushing, since Uncle Achmeth wants us to be ready on a particular day.

Brad and I feel proud. We've made it across the Atlantic without any serious problems. It's been a memorable walk in the park with Walky. Now, I am looking forward to docking in the United States. I'll need to activate some serious contacts there, because we have been without internet since we left South Africa.

Once in the States, we need new SIM cards for our phones, and I need to print my book once, just cheaply in a copy shop or so, because soon it will be the time of "to be or not to be:", and it will be handed over to a big number in the movie industry... hopefully!

In Parnaiba, north of Fortaleza, we make use of our last dirty dollars from Brad's uncle, and do a last grocery shopping before we set sail past the Caribbean. Our cash flow still looks okay, but the States will be more expensive. It is not third world with fish barbecues at a beach in New York, and I will have to kick ass to get hold of people in the movie industry. I've thought about this meeting a lot, and wonder how often they get bothered and approached. It is not going to be easy, but what was easy so far? If it was easy, too many would do similar things.

Brad and I are just lucky, that we are free and with no responsibilities other than to look after ourselves. That is a big treasure to have: no worries about kids, or grannies, house or land, cats or dogs. No, we are free, and I damn hope it will stay that way.

I also need to think of a safe escape if we need to do the firework. This must be one hundred percent organized, and fast. We'll have to get a jet ski, but where to go then? I will have to make a plan once we are in a marina there. It will take time, and time is getting short. It is nearly the middle of August today, although I wouldn't know the date. I've really lost the feeling for time. Lovely if one can do that.

I'm glad that we have strong wind. By now we know perfectly how to handle Walky at full speed, and we do fifteen knots an hour. That is perfect, speeding up north, hoping that the wind and conditions stay as they are. I believe we are lucky again, and do things an experienced sailor might not do, but we just don't know better, like the bumble bee. After all the calculations of scientists, a bumble bee is not supposed to be able to fly, but she doesn't know about these calculations and just keeps on flying. Lovely.

When I see all the beautiful bays we have to pass, and when I see all the Caribbean islands we are not allowed to visit during this mission.

I really want to go on a sailing trip again. This time we cheated too often, using our engine as soon the wind was not on our side. Of course, this wasn't supposed to be a cruise, just a transfer of our cannon boat, and it is thanks to our big engine and big tanks, and our cash flow, that most of the way we could use motor power to make it in time. But, the next time I get to this beautiful spot of the world by boat, it will be purely leisure and fun without end, damn sure about that. Now it is work, no holiday, but if pay-day comes... then in future life will always be like a holiday.

Meanwhile, Harry arrives in Nairobi the same day. Planless as he is, he doesn't have an idea of where to look for me. Even though he's got a picture and my name, Nairobi is big, and he doesn't have any further information about whether we have ever left Kenya, or where we've gone to. He reads about the well-known camping ground and takes a taxi there for a visit. He approaches the staff there with my picture, but the staff at these places changes often. They are usually backpackers who are broke, and who work there for bed and food until they have some cash and can move on again.

But George, the barkeeper, remembers me from the picture, because I always tipped George well. Nevertheless, it is only after Harry pulls out a hundred dollar note that he starts talking and tells Harry that we bought a car with Mozambican number plates, and that we gave two beautiful girls a lift, and that it was more than a month ago. He was sure that we would be in Mozambique by now.

Harry feels good. He is following in our foot prints. He uses his friends in the CIA to get some information about our whereabouts in Mozambique, but they can't help him. The infrastructure and administration in Mozambique is just too bad. That's why so many outlaws can take a dive there, and feel safe.

While passing the Caribbean in a big circle, we are hit by strong thunder, even with warm rain, and it takes some days to calm down. We are totally exhausted. I'm glad that Brad doesn't get seasick anymore; this would have killed him.

It takes our last energy reserves – three days with no sleep, with full concentration on boat and sea. Nevertheless, we are moving forward, and after each storm calm has to come. When the storm stops we are already level with the Bahamas. In maybe one or two day's more, we can dock somewhere in Miami, or even in Fort Lauderdale. Then it's welcome to America – and a hardcore test for Brad's faked passport.

If he gets through there, than his is definitely better than a real one, as promised.

And, just as I'd thought a few months ago, when I arrived in Afghanistan, I think now: when will I ever leave here again... and how? This is not a real contract job. This is quite a unique mission, full of wishful thinking!

Back in Kenya, Harry the journalist gets info from an agent that William flew one day to Beira, and then back to Pemba. So he takes the next flight to Pemba. He is on a mission, although he hasn't got a clue who he is dealing with. He books into a resort, and goes ahead with inquiries, the picture of me in his hand. He's not very successful the first days, but he doesn't give up. With typical journalist fever, he wants his story. These guys are a different bunch of people. If they smell a story, they follow like a dog, and his awful fat nose brings him to the camp of the Australian guy, and there he gets an answer to his questions: that we were there, with a fancy Land Rover that had a huge Mercedes engine, and two Italian beauties, but that we left for Beira, where we bought a burned out boat...

Now that we are close to Miami's coastline, we've even got internet again, and are checking in for marinas and harbours, and immigration. I hope that the Nautical officers are a bit cooler than the US airport officials are known to be.

We manage to get into Fort Lauderdale yacht harbour. Oh dear, we get too much attention here. I guess that with a hundred million dollar yacht nobody would turn his head, but our nutshell, with a bamboo-fixed beam, gets quite some attention.

The story now is that we spent quite some time in Brazil, between the thousand islands, and had some trouble. But we are busy because we must hit the immigration office. I even shave and put on clean clothes. They are very uncomfortable, but it will make a better impression in this glamour world. I guess that most of these huge yachts don't ever get further than to the Caribbean; they are just swimming luxury holiday houses.

There are quite a number of forms that we have to fill in, and too many stupid questions: where are we going from here, how long do we intend to stay in the US, and so on and so on. Well, I am a master in answering stupid questions with stupid answers. They make us sign up insurance for our boat, which we have to pay in cash up front, a rip off at two and a half thousand dollars. What a waste of money, but a must to be allowed to get in. Since it looks a bit dingy that we don't even have a credit card, they send some officers with dogs to our boat. That is another test: if the dogs are trained on old East German mines, or any kind of explosives, they will go mad. Then one of the officers spots our V8 in the little boat, and starts laughing. He's never seen anything like that, and such a interesting professional installation.

"Heavy on fuel?" he asks.

"Yes," I admit, "if I take it to the limit. That is why we've got these massive tanks in the back."

"Oh yes, okay." He had been wondering what we'd got there. "Give me a ride on it one day, guys."

"Sure, sir. It will only be a pleasure," I say.

Then the crew and the happy dogs leave our cannon boat, and I take a deep breath. It still takes another half an hour for all the formalities, but then we are officially in the big country of the United States of America.

Brad can't believe it, and it all looks as he was shown months ago on his iPad in the desert!

Even though we dock at class E, which is the cheapest, and always a huge walk, the parking fees for our boat are crazy. Who do they think we are? But we won't be here for long. We've still got lots to do.

I'd hoped that such a huge and well known marina would have the best immigration officers, and it seems, thank heavens, that it does. At last we are in the country of our final destination.

Brad goes mad here. In Miami he now sees everything that blew his mind the first days after he got his iPad, for real. There are the best and biggest yachts, and there are the hottest cars parked, and there are the most beautiful girls. This is the American dream, to have a yacht in Fort Lauderdale, and to catch the gorgeous girls, no matter what they've got in their heads.

I do need at least another two days to get my book ready for print, because I have to implement a wishful thinking happy end, that will be good for America and the rest of the world. I do not want to get too far into politics. I just want to give a wakeup call, and might even change history with it! I've thought of the finish all the time, but now, by putting it into words, I can see it like a movie in front of me, and believe that it could happen for real… as real as I've lived through the book till now. And, if it doesn't happen in reality, then let it happen in a very, very realistic action movie, please! But God, Allah and the universe will decide.

I write the finish with a smile and a bottle of Scotch. It didn't even take two hours since I'd spent so much time already thinking about how the story would have to end. I feel that I've found the perfect ending; actually quite wonderful. Lovely!

I am once again impressed by my fantasy and imagination. How it all comes together, step by step, with a bit of humour mixed in, but at the end of the day with a very serious message for those who've got the power to change things in this world for the better.

In one way or another, this message will get known.

I receive a stunning cover for the book, made by a very good friend in South Africa and done exactly according to my instructions. I save everything on memory stick, which I will take to a big copy shop, where I can print it on my own, unseen by anyone.

My friends promise me some interesting meetings with important people in the movie industry, but by now I want one of the best, or the best, to do it.

It seems, however, he is difficult to get hold of, but I know a lot of his successful movies. That man has the guts, and the power, to make the movie as I visualize it. That's no one else than the famous Steven Spielberg. I need to meet him. Five minutes will be enough, and he will be my man. If necessary, I will have to travel to Los Angeles, to Hollywood, but time is getting short, and our budget is being eaten up too fast, here in the United States.

I really beg my friends to get me his contact details, or any info about how to get hold of him. He must be around, socially or on business, and there must be people who know where he moves. That info is all I need to get my way.

After I print my book, and hold it all in my hands, and read and read it all over again, I am more convinced of its success than ever, and believe that it makes sense.

I see it as the masterpiece of my creative fantasy.

Good friends pay out sooner or later, and I get a call from my sexy friend, Sally. She met someone who works closely with Steven, and now I know that he will be coming to New York in the next days for a function. Okay, that's something. But where will he be? Nobody knows. I need more info, please. This girl must know who to ask. Come on guys, get clever, get your connections going, and find out for me. Nobody understands why I am so under pressure, but I cannot tell anybody... not yet.

And here I get another clap on my shoulder.

"STOP it!" Brad screams. He hasn't done it for a while, but he is still reading my moods like a book.

What, at this stage and time, does Brad want to happen? Born in Afghanistan, and being Moslem and faithful to his people and their beliefs and culture, what does he want to happen?

To have a part in the movie to come?

Or to be part of something close to a terror attack?

I want to talk to him about this issue. I need clarity, because soon I have to prepare our "cracker" and we will both know what the explosive number will be to start the firework.

To get him on a high, so that he opens up totally, I hire a Ferrari for us, a red Ferrari convertible. I know that this is his dream car. And, even though he doesn't have a driver's license, I will give him a go behind the wheel. The car hire guy asks quite some cash, and a high cash deposit from us. I don't feel like putting the soldier's credit cards down here; I am very sure they are all hot now.

If we damage the car, we will be left with only two thousand dollars, and we still need to get to New York. We cruise the boulevards. Yes, we feel like Miami Vice, except that we are better, we are cooler, but nobody knows that yet, hahahaah.

Before we have too much alcohol at one of the hottest beach bars in Miami, I ask him, "Brad, my dear best friend, what is your wish? What do you wish to happen in the next days?"

"Look, William, I am thankful for every day, every hour, I've experienced with you. I feel reborn. All plans are from you, and I will further do as always, as promised. I will do as you say, and what you want me to do. Whatever we get out, we share as we discussed before we left. And I feel like you, now that I lived it through life: your book and movie will be done, I have no doubt, like all the other stuff we got done successfully, and now the end will be fine too, my friend.

"We are not terrorists, we are good people, and with the movie we shall get the same results sooner or later, as by executing Walky's firework!"

This are exactly my thoughts too. I'm glad!

"Okay... now we celebrate this. We are still on the same line and same mission!"

We have a feast, plenty of beer and cognac, and forget the time. Yes we celebrate as if all were already done, but we did need the pressure-relief that evening. We haven't partied since Beira, and that's ten thousand miles away.

After we pay he asks for the car keys. Oh my Lord, can I say no now? He promises me that if he gets caught, I can go ahead and finish the mission alone. Hmmmm, that is true... and here we go, he behind the steering wheel of nearly four hundred horse power, a bit drunk, as I am. God and Allah be with us. Wild boys still do crazy things like that.

We've only got a few miles to go, mostly straight. It is a hot night in Miami, and we would love to have some weeks of party here; next time we will. Brad does well. He only had a few lessons in our Landy, but he had a good instructor!

I am very relieved when we get to the Marina, park the sportster nicely, and can walk to our swimming home. What a lovely day it has been, and would have still been if a scrummy noise was not interfering with the romantic silence. As I turn around, I see the Ferrari rolling down towards the jetty, getting faster and faster.

"Braaaddd, you forget the hand brake!"

"Oh... hand brake," he mumbles. I try to reach the car, but there's no chance. There it goes down the quay and comes to a peaceful standstill on the sundeck of a three-mast sailing yacht.

That's trouble... big trouble. I run back, and I tell Brad we need to go now.

"Where to?"

"To New York. It's time to introduce you to a very important... lady!"

Let's go. Now we go for victory. Yes, this seems a good moment to leave Miami and head towards New York, which is still twelve hundred miles away, and now it is already early morning of the 8th of September.

We untie Walky, I start the V8, and off we shoot out into the night. The fresh breeze will wake me up, although the downfall of the Ferrari has already done that pretty well. The car should be insured, but our deposit of five thousand dollars cash is lost and we are down to two thousand dollars. It's time for pay-day! Shit, shit, shit... this shouldn't have happened, but I had needed a kick to leave here and to go on to our final destination!

And this dumb little accident has just kicked our butts nicely out of here; another call from the universe.

Brad is fast asleep. No wonder. I will let him get a few hours, and then I need to crash for a bit. I keep myself busy with my checklist. I am still waiting for info about where to find Steven S.

And I have to get the boat ready. In case we let off the firework, the escape will be as follows: when the tide is right and before sunrise, I need to get Walky in the right position, which I've calculated and measured plenty of times with an endless number of internet pictures of the target, and reports around it. All must go very quickly. I know we will be seen by someone. But we can use the chaos around the target, after execution.

To set off the firework, Brad will pick me up from the boat with a hired jet ski, from where I will dial the number of a cell phone that is connected to the TNT load on Walky. We'll return to shore by the shortest distance, where we will have a motorbike waiting. Immediately, we will board a cruise liner to Cuba, which will leave early that morning, September eleven. We will check in at around lunchtime the day before. Once in Cuba, we will have to make new plans, and follow up the outcome.

So that is my plan so far. May God and Allah, and my army of guardian angels, be with us!

Meanwhile, that day Harry arrives in Beira, also a bit disappointed by this once beautiful coastal holiday town. But this sniffing dog won't give up. Our famous pub invites him for lunch, but, before he gives attention to the menu, his eyes are hit by a poster on the wall, promoting the "Church of Landmines"!

On the poster are Thomas, Brad and myself, and a map of how to find the place.

So, there's no time for lunch this day. He wants to get there as soon as he possibly can, and makes a deal with a taxi driver.

Back in the USA, my oldest problem hits my head: the financial bit. We are down to two thousand dollars, and will have to pay these horrendous harbour fees again. Well, not for long maybe. Oh dear, worries, worries, worries – and a half drunken, sleepy Brad who doesn't get me out of this mood.

I go through my plan once again, not knowing if my cannon will have enough power to hit the target on the right spot. I need to get Walky at a good angle, and as close as possible, before I dial the explosive numbers. I will have three capsules connected to three cell phones in the load, which gives me two spare numbers to dial in case one doesn't work. The numbers are all saved in my and Brad's cell phones, in case we need to do what we've planned for so long now. The thought gets my mind cracking. What a mission to accomplish! I can't believe it is all so close, and real.

My phone rings, and it is Sally. Oh, this sweet talking doll. She just doesn't have a talent for making a long story short.

"Hi, what's new, where will Steven stay?"

"Oh, darling, why are you screaming, what is that noise," blah, blah, blah.

"Baby, I'm going at thirty knots in the direction of New York. We fucked up a rented car in Miami, long story... I'll tell you later. So, tell me, any news, and any more information?"

"Yes, my lover boy, he will stay in the Hilton Hotel in Manhattan, and will have to join the government function for the memorial of September eleven ten years ago. You know what happened that day?"

"Oh yes, sweetheart, I do remember... very, very well. So, you're confident this information is accurate?"

"Yes, just trust me. I got it from his closest friends."

"Oh Sally, you are a darling. This is very important to me. I owe you!"

"Oh yes, you do. When are you coming to LA? If you promise to visit me, I might even tell you his suite number!"

"Sure, sure... next month, big promise. I will see you either as the gypsy I am now, or as a rich man. So, what's the number, sweetheart?"

"Suite 788, and you'd better visit me my boy. You are rich already,

all the others only got money!

"Hmmm... charming wise words! Thank you so much, I will visit you, big promise! It all depends on Steven now."

"Okay, and then you'll tell me the full story?

"Yes, I will – or you can read my book, or keep your TV on. I have to go now... chat soon, my sweetheart, mwwaahh!"

Aaaoouuww, that was the best call ever. I will find Steven Spielberg at this hotel. That's my first priority now!

As the sun and a lovely breeze come up, I wake Brad to set the sail, so that we can save fuel. He is hang over, poor boy, but I cannot feel sorry for him now. He apologizes for the accident of forgetting the handbrake, and I just tell him that that was yesterday, and we will sort it all out later.

I share the good news that I got a hint about where to find the big moviemaker, and that makes him smile too. He has to take over the boat so that I take can get some sleep now... sharing is caring. I think I'll only be able to sleep because of the alcohol, and because I have been on my feet for thirty hours. If it weren't for these factors, my brain wouldn't switch off.

Meanwhile, Harry arrives at the forgotten village behind Tete, and walks to the church of landmines. Some backpackers are around, visiting this sad place, another witness of a battle where innocent civilians had to pay the price of a stupid war with their lives.

Cheeky as he is, he approaches Thomas with a nice donation of a few hundred dollars, and starts questioning, about the whole story behind the church, in order to cosy up to Thomas before he inquires about me. Thomas likes talking, and shares what he knows: that we built a boat, and that we wanted to sail to America for a big party in September.

"Oh, is that so?" Yes, and Thomas tells him how proud he is of me, and what good guys we are, and what we have done for the village. He even tells Harry that we took away two drums of mines on our last visit. No, he didn't question us about it, but is sure we needed them for promotion purpose. There's nothing to worry about.

"They took mines away from here, from the grave yard?"

"Yes, they filled up two old oil drums. Oh, I wish I were that young and healthy again," Thomas starts.

So Harry's got the info he needs, even if he is confused and doesn't know how to take it, and he makes his way back to Beira. There, in his hotel, he receives mail from his friend the CIA agent: my full CV, and my military experience and education about explosives.

In our Pub he gets more info from the drunken farmer, about how funnily and primitively we equipped the boat, and that he thought us crazy to risk our lives for a party in New York. For the same price we could have flown to the States.

An old fisherman adds an even funnier story. "They might have never made it," he says. He's heard a funny story about how they got attacked by pirates, but somehow some explosion on their boat sank the pirates' speed boat, and only one guy survived...

Now Harry's mind gets busy, very busy, and even more worried than my brain was at the same time. But, when he forwards the information he's got to his CIA friend, he only gets laughter from the other end of the telephone line

"Hhhahahahaha, what a story, a shepherd and a gypsy sank a pirate boat? Hahahahaha, wonderful! And next, the Statue of Liberty or what?"

We are sailing into the night. We are both very quiet, and for a change I could shout at Brad to stop worrying, but I don't. We've both got all rights to be extremely nervous.

Next morning we can make out the impressive skyline of Manhattan. How peaceful and quiet the city looks from afar, but in reality it is a city, with nearly a hundred kilometres of coastline, that never sleeps.

It is the 9th of September, and I have to start with last preparations for the firework, and adjust another loaded steel frame around our engine. I will put the capsules into the load only after we've docked, otherwise it will be just too dangerous.

We sail straight to the pier in front of Manhattan. While I tie up Walky at the pier, my hands start to shiver, but I ignore it since I know my body and mind, and I've programmed myself for forty-eight hours of full concentration, as I did in special training in the army.

We have some fish and chips, and a Coke – no alcohol anymore... or should we? Then I let Brad discover the city, while I make my way to the Hilton Hotel, where I sit down in the lounge for a coffee, and observe the busy atmosphere. I cannot sit here for days waiting for Steven Spielberg. My nerves won't be able to tolerate that, and there must be another way.

I go to the reception and ask if they have a room available.

"No sir, we have only suites. For how many days?"

"Oh. How much is a suite for two young men?"

'We have a special on for six hundred and eighty-five dollars, excluding breakfast, and the mini-bar will be charged extra."

Oh, what a bargain...! My goodness.

"Do you have a suite high up? I love the view over to Liberty Island."

"Sorry, sir, we are nearly fully occupied. Oh, excuse me, I just got a cancellation in, suite 795 will be available and has a lovely view."

"Well, then that shall be my home for the next two days," I agree with a smile, but I cry inside about the money. But it might be the last investment for our mission.

"Can I please have your passport and credit card?"

I hand over my passport, and say, "I'm afraid that the credit card is the reason that I am stuck here for two days. My jacket with my cards got stolen yesterday night in a bar. Luckily, we sailors always keep cash for emergencies on the boat."

I receive the keys and make my way up to suite 795, while I check where Stevens' suite 788 is located. It is obviously just further down the long corridor. I step out on the balcony of our suite, and count the windows to suite 788. I can sit here and wait until the light goes on, and then I will find my way to him for a chat. I will, whatever it takes!

As I am standing on this balcony and observing Liberty Island about two miles away, I remember home in Cape Town. There we also see an island two miles away in the bay, Robben Island, which is a museum today, and a witness of the past, and proof of how strong people can be if they never give up.

This island is a very big part of South Africa's history, used for decades as prison for political prisoners, before former inmate Nelson Mandela became President of South Africa. This man is a legend, and the biggest hero, not only all over Africa. He enjoys respect all over the world. He walked the talk. Because he was fighting for, and believing in, the rights of African people, he did a long, long, very long walk to freedom.

THE FINAL COUNTDOWN

I meet up with Brad at the boat a few hours later, and tell him the good news that we will stay in a luxury five star hotel, and the bad news that we are down to less than three hundred dollars. He answers with a look high up to heaven, and then we pack our stuff and, in the last minutes, I switch on the cell phones and connect them to the electric capsules in Walky's load. The next time I put my feet on this boat it will be for only a short, but fast, ride of not even three miles.

I close my eyes for a few seconds, and walk away with Brad. We decide to get at least one bottle of Scotch, and I introduce him to our luxury suite.

He loves it. He says it looks like in *Pretty Woman*, one of his favourite movies. He must have watched hundreds of films by now, but is convinced that if our story gets done it will be one of the best movies ever made. I take this as a compliment, and wish to hear the same words from Steven Spielberg in the next thirty hours. That would make me the happiest man on earth.

We stretch our legs out on our double beds, and switch on the TV, trying to relax. Brad discovers the mini bar, which has more items available than any supermarket in Mozambique. I tell him to leave it, since we cannot afford the stuff.

He hits my forehead, and starts laughing, shaking his head.

"My dear friend William. In two days we can either buy a suite here, or we will be sitting on a cruise to Cuba, or not?"

He is right. Yes, he is damn right. Gosh, this boy is more clear in his head than I am, very impressive. I am proud of him, and I grab an eleven dollar Heineken out of the fridge.

On the TV the movie *The Jackal* with Bruce Willis starts, one of my favourite movies. I loved his detailed plan – not what he planned, but how he planned.

Why do they eliminate a single person only in movies? Why don't they use, in reality, highly educated and trained seals to get a dictator or a terror leader out of their country with a one shot mission, as planned by Bruce Willis. Why must a land like the United States invade a whole country with a whole army? Do presidents never watch movies? Instead they listen to officers who grew up and got trained with computers and war games, and have never been in real combat.

The beer is good for me, as usual, but I jump up every minute, to see if there is light in suite 788, or if, at least, the curtains are open, but there is nothing so far. I do hope that the information from Sally was correct. If not, I might squat in her lovely villa at Malibu Beach in California for a few days, while I hunt other movie maker.

But enough "ifs" and "whens". This thing is good and will work, and I help myself to a little Remy Martin out of our mini bar. Lovely.

Bruce Willis gets caught because he is known by the authorities. That was the only weak point in his calculations. Brad and myself, we are nobodies – no names, no criminal record at all, if you don't count a few fancy speed tickets in SA – so nobody is looking for us, or is curious about what we are up to. That thought relaxes me, and I enjoy a little afternoon snooze.

Meanwhile, our Harry is already at Johannesburg airport, trying to get to New York. That's a long, long journey, even by plane, since there are hardly any direct flights.

But, hobby detective that he is, he activates all the connections and friends he has online. He wants to know if a trimaran, with the name *Walk the Talk*, has been seen anywhere around New York, or if this boat is even lying somewhere in a marina.

And, if this is the case, he suggests that they should have a closer look at it.

He even tries to get the New York police department suspicious, but they are receiving hundreds of tip offs like this by the hour this day, and there is really no time or manpower to chase two crazy adventurers who have sailed from Mozambique to New York.

They file the call, and will follow up if there is time. That's their duty.

But for the next two days, with all kinds of international leaders and politicians attending functions in New York, they are booked out. The security measures in and around New York are on high alert, the up coming date of September the 11th might be chosen for further terrorist attacks. There's no time for credit card thieves...

I wake up with a shock. I might have missed Steven checking in! I run to the balcony, but there are no changes yet. It is already evening and the city lights are up. What an amazing city this is. More people live in one square mile here, than in a whole Afghanistan city!

I have a shower and freshen up. I don't want to look like a beggar if I meet Steven. Brad asks if we're going out for dinner, and I throw him the room service menu.

"Same payment procedure as the Mini bar... go mad, my boy!"

And at last there is light in suite 788! I run out into the corridor, but there is no one on the floor. Every door is closed. The elevator opens and a housekeeper comes out. I stay in front of 788, and ask if my Uncle Steven, the gentleman in suite 788, has arrived, and I point to the door.

"Yes sir, he did. I just picked up his tuxedo to get pressed."

"Oh, that's my uncle, always in a tuxedo." We laugh together, and he adds that he's already got a fifty dollar tip, because the gentleman needs his tuxedo back in the next half an hour. I keep on smiling at him and walk back to my room. Taking that tuxedo back will be my chance to get access to his room, and at least a few minutes for a talk, although now all the first sentences I've had ready for this talk are gone from my mind. How was I supposed to start the talk? Damn, but it will come as it comes.

I grab the printout of my book, and place myself in the corridor. This is the moment I have been waiting for, for a long time. How many times have I smiled and laughed about the idea of confronting this big moviemaker with my book. How many times have I mentioned it to my friends and have got a cheeky comment back. Now it all seems to be happening. I do not expect an answer immediately, but do hope for at least some attention and acknowledgement.

Hope he doesn't treat me like all the negative people I've approached in South Africa as possible investors for all kind of business ideas – fantastic business ideas, but too much for their imaginations, and most of these investors are full of shit, and not really interested in helping someone else get on his feet, even if they liked my ideas. I believe that I always got stuck because I didn't even have one percent of the amount needed for any business.

This business, I mean my movie proposal, is a different approach, and if Steven is as the media always advertises, then he will show some interest. Well, he better checks my manuscript!

The housekeeper comes again, and I cross to him and hand him another fifty dollar tip. Without any further questions he hands over Steven's tuxedo – I mean, of course, my uncle's tuxedo – and I knock on his door. I knock again. Nothing happens… my nerves… my words on my tongue… open that damn door… and now Steven Spielberg, half naked just in shorts, opens the door. I walk in with a big step and close the door behind me, while he starts looking in his bag for some tip money.

I take the chance and start talking.

"Mr. Spielberg, I apologize. I am not the housekeeper, and I am not a criminal either. I just want to talk to you." While I say this I block the hotel's panic button at the wall. "Please, it won't take more than five minutes, and then I'll go."

He keeps calm and sits down, and answers that this is exactly the time he needs to finish the whisky he's just poured.

"So, young man, how can I help you?"

I am nearly speechless, but my heartbeat wakes me up.

"Sir, I wrote a lovely book, a very adventurous story, which I think is made to be turned in a movie." He starts laughing.

"Yes sir, I didn't expect any other reaction from you, and I can imagine how many people approach you with their stories, but I believe that you have the kind of character that will make you at least a bit curious about each of them."

Now he looks bored and downs his drink. I add that this story is different, and that it might change the future of America.

"That would be wonderful," he says. "How is that supposed to happen?"

Now, he cannot stop me talking, and in two minutes I explain, in short sentences, the content. His face changes, and he looks me more deeply in the eyes. I put down my printout, which has my contact number and email. I beg him to have a look at it in the next twenty-four hours, and say that it is very important.

Now he laughs again, and tells me how busy he is.

Now I play my joker: I show him a newspaper from South Africa, the Cape Times, from 13th of September 2001. In it is a cartoon, in which he, Steven Spielberg, was approached earlier, to make a movie called: *Plane Crash into the World Trade Centre*! And how he pushes it aside, with the comment: Too much fantasy involved!

"Please sir, take some time to read my book. I believe strongly in you, and if you decide to my disappointment, then please consider playing your short important role in the movie, because you are already part of it, even though it might be produced by someone else, who will get famous then!"

He stares at the title and picture on the cover, and then he reads the content described on the back.

Then I try to be clever, and move a contract over to him and say, "Thank you for your time, sir. I know I am very cheeky, but so far I've got what I want. And I leave in the strong hope that you like the story and what I've done. That's the price, and all rights for a possible movie are yours, if you decide positive!" And I hold a pen for him. He flies over the ten liner, which includes my Thailand bank details, and he signs this document of first option with another laugh. Maybe he does it only to get rid of me.

I don't laugh. My face is serious, and I quickly think whether I've said everything that needs to be said. I feel good. This was a very important step. I get up with the words, "You are American. You should care even more than I do. I will wait for your call tomorrow," and I walk towards the door. Then he asks for my name. I tell him, and mention that all my details are in the book I've given him. There's even a copy of my passport.

Then he shakes my hand, and says thank you, he will have a look at it, but he cannot promise that he'll find the time to read it in the next twenty-four hours.

"Well," I say, "if that is the case, then you don't have to read it anymore."

"What do you mean by that?" he asks.

"Read it. You will find the answers in the book. Sorry, I've over done it with your time by five minutes already," and I walk out of his room and close the door behind me. In the corridor I make a big jump. Damn, that was cool. What a good talk, and I have a strong feeling I've awoken his interest.

Back in our room I tell Brad how it went, and that I am sure we will hear from Steven, and that for today our job is done. Then someone knocks on our door. I look at Brad, but he just smiles and jumps up to open it. Oh, my dear, here it comes. Three waiters carry in a feast fit for an army: lobster, turkey, salads and all kind of snacks. Brad tips them, as he has learned to do from his movies.

"Did I see right?" I exclaim. "You tipped them a hundred dollars?"

"Yes, William, I did. It might be the first and last time I ever tip in a five star hotel, so I thought I'd do it right!" High five, and we start with our buffet. Lovely!

Oh, what a feast, with even a bottle of South African shiraz. Compare this to our evenings at the campfire, with doggy bags from my kitchen and tea. Even the fact that we are now down to a hundred dollars can't bother me!

Then I get another email from Uncle Achmeth:

"We are awaiting your attendance at the public holiday coming up, looking forward to another unforgettable event!"

I take a deep breath. What shall I answer? I am a bit drunk, so I reply:

"The roast is in the oven, waiting for the signal and the celebration will begin!"

Now we make another toast and turn up the music. We are on track, and we have perfect timing. We empty the bottle of champagne on our balcony, enjoying a hot late-summer night in New York, and I pray to God – and, it seems, he to Allah – that we will have many, many more of these evenings.

Meanwhile, our friend Harry checks onto a flight to London and a connecting flight to New York. He is on fire to get his story, and he just might.

We sleep into the day, have our left over buffet for breakfast, and keep the "Do Not Disturb" sign outside the room door. We are happy here. There are still plenty of drinks in the mini bar, and the food should last another day. We will need this lazy day to get ready for the final countdown.

We sit on the floor, while a news channel runs in the background, repeating all kind of reports and interviews from ten years ago, when the world was shaken by the terror attack, when the World Trade Centre, here in New York, collapsed after being hit by hijacked airplanes, which turns into the biggest disaster the world has ever seen.

And how a stressed-out President George Bush announces a war against terror! That primitive cowboy!

Brad and I try to chill, and we go through our plan again. The question of whether we are doing the right thing is not allowed to come up anymore. Now it is all lined up, and we have to finish what we've started, in the hope that the right people will get the message:

That they have to finish, or it may be better to say that they have to end, what they have started!

My hope is that not one human being will be harmed and, according to the information I've got, there shouldn't be any people close to our target between six and seven in the morning, and if there are, then let God be with them.

We book in on the cruise liner that is supposed to leave the next day to Cuba. Whether we will really be on board then, only God knows.

Brad sits there, like he did a few months ago, but he is not watching fancy pics and movies about America. Now he is watching the travel movies that he took and put on his iPad. Nice short movies from Bangkok, game viewing in Kenya, beach parties in Mombasa, country roads in Tanzania, and the big job in Mozambique.

There is plenty of material for more books, and input for the movie that I wish to get produced about the goal I am expecting to reach by doing what might need to be done next morning. With one eye and ear always on my cell phone I wait to see if the big movie producer who stays down the corridor will contact me, but the phone stays silent.

The idea to visit him again doesn't get into action.

I believe the talk I had with Steven was good, and I made it quite clear, what I expect from him if he is interested.

Meanwhile, Steven Spielberg in suite 788 takes the movie proposal this morning while he has his tea, and he reads it through. He gets hooked on the story, otherwise he would have put it aside after a few minutes. Instead, he is late for his lunch appointment.

Back from lunch, he finishes the book and he takes off his glasses and wipes his eyes, which have been stuck on the last page. He moves his head. No, he doesn't shake his head, he moves his head, as if he is talking to himself. He gets up, opens his balcony door and stands at the railing, looking over to Liberty Island for a few minutes, and then he goes back and reads the last chapter again. He seems speechless, but he has nobody to talk to anyway. At last he puts the booklet into his suitcase, and doesn't leave it with the other magazines on his coffee table.

How two guys in suite 795 would love to know what he is thinking, but their phones stay silent the whole day.

Every time I turn totally silent and look at a wall, Brad wakes me up. He is as convinced as it gets that it all will be fine. He is not nervous at all. He is only nervous about what all he will do and buy if a pay-day becomes reality.

So that issue keeps us busy, and we paint out what we will do with a few million dollars. My dream stays: I want a little farm in Africa, my vegetable garden, game and domestic animals, a lovely farm house with a huge fireplace, a beautiful view, and an outside bath on the lawn. Brad's wishes are different. He wants that penthouse in Thailand, where he can party day and night, and go to lovely beaches on a motorbike.

Well, these dreams can hopefully come true very soon; lovely dreams.

By late afternoon, the wines and beers are finished in the mini bar, and we turn to the harder spirits. I feel relaxed – damn alcohol – but I also know that I can still do my job in the morning. We will crash into our beds early if we keep on drinking like this.

I turn the ringtone of my cell to maximum volume. I can't miss an important call which might still come.

On the TV they show all the memorials to come the next day. The biggest will be held at Ground Zero, where the World Trade Centre once stood.

The scenes of how the airplanes hit the Twin Towers is repeated by the hour, as it was ten years ago. How could something like that happen? How many years of planning were behind it? And then a helpless President Bush, who had to come up with something. It had taken quite a while before all TV channels could broadcast the speech and statement of the most powerful man in the world, the President of the United States.

George Bush had to stop reading a book, *The Pet Goat*, with second-graders, when it happened, and had to deal with this event immediately. The United States has got plans for all kinds of crises and attacks, filed with an action plan, but in the face of this kind of attack, which was immediately broadcast to the whole world, what can a man, president or not, say in a speech to calm his nation, and the rest of the world, down? America's pride got hurt so strongly, not to forget the thousands of innocent victims who were killed in and around the Twin Towers, and in the planes that hit with such deadly effect. Various theories came up afterwards. In a 2008 poll in seventeen countries, fifteen percent of those surveyed believed the US government was responsible for the attacks, seven percent believed Israel was and another seven percent believed that some perpetrator other than Al Qaeda, was responsible. The poll found that respondents in the Middle East were more likely to name a perpetrator other than Al Qaeda.

The president doesn't have any doubt: this was an act of terror, and the United States of America is not going to stand still and take attacks like that without reaction. So, to prevent things like this from ever happening again, he announces the "War against Terror!"

This is a big thing to say, and who are they to start? Where are the terrorists? How many are there? They can be close and far!

There is hardly a route to follow the people responsible for and behind it. This is not a huge bank robbery, where one can close up an area and check every house and car. Terrorists can be anywhere, even where you would never expect them, even in your own house…so where do you want to have your war, Mr. Bush?

Well, I admit that I cannot recall all the theories myself, nor am I able to discuss any possible theories of who and why a particular group arranged the downfall of the Twin Towers, so I am not going to mention phrases and reports. This all happened years ago, and most people involved now in this crazy war have already forgotten the reasons.

But I do remember that a high number of people, even in Germany, believed that it was an inside job by the United States government. If that was the case, which might never be proven, then it's even more high time to stop this useless war in Afghanistan. As I said, we cannot turn back time, but we can influence strongly the future, and that is what we might possibly achieve with our mission and our cannon boat. We will not start another war; we want a war to end!

I have to go down to get some cigarettes. We do not want any service staff to enter our Camp 795. When I rush back to our suite, I nearly run over Steven. Gosh, I hadn't expected him at all. He speaks to me. He asks how long we will still be in New York. I hadn't expected any further talks or even questions from him, and with some alcohol in my blood, I said that we are more or less timeless, and that we came with a boat.

"You came with a boat!?" he repeats.

Now I wake up. "Yes, Mr. Spielberg, we came with a boat, all the way from Mozambique."

"From Beira," he throws in, which makes me smile. He must have read the book.

"Yes, correct, from Beira!" And I wish him a nice evening, and speed up back to our room.

I tell Brad about the short conversation, and that I am happy to know that Steven must have read it, and I am wondering now why I chickened out of a longer talk on the corridor. My inner brain must have been scared of further questions, and, well, Steven knows where to contact me, if he needs more information. I liked his surprised face, when I told him that we came with a boat.

I do a last briefing with Brad, who is already bored by doing this. I must have gone through our plan too often with him, and he can finish any sentence I start. Which at least means that he knows exactly what our next day's job is. We have a last whiskey, and we hit our beds. I fall asleep with my phone in my hand. I've set the alarm clock for five o'clock in the morning.

With a strong consciousness that I am not really doing anything bad, I fall into a deep sleep and do not witness the strong storm and bad weather that are coming up outside.

FIREWORK WITH A MESSAGE

Journalist Harry must have arrived in New York during the night, to find further info in an email from his CIA friend that I'd entered the United States a few days ago at the marina in Fort Lauderdale. He learns that they do not have any further info about where we went to.

But he also gets hold of the ugly fat guy from whom we'd rented the Ferrari.

Harry has a long talk with him. It is quite difficult to get any further information from him, since he won't stop swearing and saying what he would do with us if he ever gets us in his clutches again, even though he will get compensated by the insurance.

Harry asked if we'd left any contact telephone numbers in the rental contract. Yes, he says, but it is unreadable to him.

"Oh, come on, get me the number," urges Harry. But old Mike can't make out the numbers that I wrote purposefully unreadable on the form.

"Try harder," screams Harry down the phone. So Mike gives him a number, not knowing if the seven might be a four, or one of the nines an eight.

"Good luck, Mr. Harry," he says, and he drops the phone. The first thing Harry feels like doing is to call up all yacht harbours around New York, asking for a trimaran by name *Walk the Talk*, and also mentioning my name. Happily, he gets the info that the boat is docked at the Manhattan Pier, where, at five thirty in the morning, Harry is nervously walking up and down, waiting to take us by surprise.

When the alarm goes off at five, I jump straight out of bed, as I would have done in the old days in the army. Brad takes a bit longer to surface, but not so long that I had to push him. His first words are that this is finally our day which will decide for our future. Yes, it is, and yes, it will. There is no missed call or message on my phone, which leaves us now with only one way of action!

I walk out with my coffee to the balcony, and see light in Steven's suite. The idea to give him a call is killed by Brad, who says that the storm is already on without our action. I look outside the window. Very true, nobody will be out at sea in this weather. This is good for us; the sea is too rough for any pleasure or day cruises to be on the water.

I take my binoculars to make sure that there are no unexpected witnesses close to our target. I see no movement around there, and I'm glad. But, as I take the binoculars from my eyes I notice something moving. It is in the sea, just a boat, but far away... crazy people.

I walk back in to get another coffee, but then a thought shoots through my head and I go back onto the balcony and look through my binoculars. I cannot find the boat anymore, the sea is so rough, with waves four metes high, I guess. But there the boat is again, and I do not want to believe my eyes. I receive Brad's favourite shout, "Stop it, William!" We need to go, but I do not react to his call at all.

He comes out to pull me in by my arm, and I scream at him, "Sorry my friend, this time I cannot stop. I cannot stop what I see!" And I hand over my binoculars.

It takes a few seconds and then he gets afraid, and turns around looking at me with big eyes. Then he shouts, "There is Walky, all on his own, out on the wild sea!" Brad only confirms what I saw.

I take my binoculars back and look at our boat. Damn, it must have come loose in the storm. We idiots didn't check on it in the last days. What now?

"Brad, get the last whiskeys."

"What?"

"Get the damn whiskeys," I shout, and he follows my order like a soldier.

Meanwhile, our friend Harry is trying to walk in the rain and storm. He knows he is close to our boat, but when he arrives at the spot where he had been told that he would find *Walk the Talk*, he only finds a broken rope. Damn, so close he was. What a pity.

Brad is back in five seconds with two whiskeys, and we down them at once. "What now?" he yells. "We must take the jet ski and get to the boat!"

I shake my head. We won't be able to see the boat from the jet ski, and first we would have to steal the jet ski. I do not think that the hire place would open up today.

I am shaking my head. How stupid I am. I should have known that it is either a woman, or the weather, that crosses plans. With me living back home at the Cape of Storms, I should have thought about a fast weather change here. But now it is too late: Walky is on his own.

I was not prepared for an incident like this, and cannot take my eyes from my binoculars. It takes a while to spot Walky, which is on course to Liberty Island, again. I wish I had put in a remote control. Surely it cannot be that this storm will sink our boat, and that everything has been for nothing.

I check my phone. There is no missed call or message. Then I unpack my laptop.

There is one mail from Uncle Achmeth:

"Bad weather in town I have been told, but this should not keep us from a party?"

I do not know what to answer and run back to the balcony, observing that our boat is nearly hundred metres closer to the island by now! The island gets washed and overrun by strong waves, which might work for us, but it is like roulette. I need Walky in a particular position to give the one and only possible one and a half tonne TNT-shot from our cannon!

But Walky could be smashed into pieces any second now. I take off the binoculars and hand them to Brad, who doesn't know what to say anymore. Me neither. But one never knows. I get my cell phone and search for the "firework" number. Pressing key three will be enough to activate one of the electric detonator capsules in Walky's cannon.

Now I realize that this is not a training exercise in the peaceful army of twenty-five years ago. This is supposed to give a message to the world, not to shoot a hole into the sea, like a dynamite fisher!

I grab the binoculars from Brad. Walky must already have been dashed against the island's surrounding wall. The beam with the bamboo is broken in the middle, the next wave could be the end. This cannot be true.

Harry is upset, and dials the number given by Mike from the car hire. It rings and rings. Then a twenty-four hour pizza service picks up the phone. Harry is losing his temper and screams, "Fuck you!" into his phone. "I need to speak to William. I don't want a damn fucking pizza!

"Sorry sir, we don't do William pizzas," and the call gets cut off.

He walks up and down shaking his head, and looks at the little piece of paper again, and thinks he will now try a four instead of a seven as the last number.

I have to witness how Walky loses the bamboo fixed beam. Damn, this boat feels like a helpless baby to me. It is lost, totally lost. Then I see a huge wave building up behind it. Damn it!

God... Allah... do something! And there it happens. The huge wave gets hold of Walky, lifts it high up and throws it against the concrete base of the Statue of Liberty. There our boat stands at ninety degrees to the sky, behind the Statue of Liberty – and will fall over backwards at any moment.

Harry is determined to find us, and is busy dialling the next number, swearing that he will take me down. He presses the key for the four. At the same second the phone slips out of his hand and he sees a giant explosion, a huge fireball at the Statue of Liberty. He sees what Brad and I see.

"What have you done?" Brad asks.

"Nothing, my friend, nothing," and I show him my empty hands.

What is happening now two miles away, like in a slow motion movie, is unbelievable. The statue seems to be hit and to shift on her heels and to have difficulty in standing up. She is shaking. The wild sea is irritating, but the proof comes quickly: the whole Statue of Liberty bends forward, in the direction of Manhattan, falling from her pedestal and going down on her knees, although the steel construction inside this massive concrete monument keeps the structure together.

This is real, and not a movie. Now the whole statue slips off her pedestal and hits the lawn with her knees. Her main body swings backwards, which breaks her neck, and the head drops forwards – down, but still attached to the body. It's not over yet. The lady's wrist seems to be broken too, and her right hand drops down. She's holding her torch now like children would hold a lantern.

I quickly close my eyes and open them again, but Brad grabs my binoculars, which I do not need anymore.

I can't see any sign of Walky, but what I can see is absolutely unbelievable: the best known American monument, the Statue of Liberty, symbol of liberty and democracy, is kneeling down on the lawn on Liberty Island, facing the ground with a shaking lantern in her right hand. My smile is coming back on my face.

"I couldn't have done it better," I say to Brad, who is still speechless. But, as he recognizes that I'm laughing tears, he joins in. We hug in the rain on the balcony and dance, as we if we have won a battle. We have not fired a single shot, but we have delivered a unique message!

Now we will get the needed attention for book and movie to come, this "event" is like a huge, worldwide free advertising, the words shall get spread and understood all over the planet. And my biggest hope is, that the President himself gets a copy of the book as soon as possible.

This all happens while Steven is having his morning tea, looking in a hurry through my book again. Then he shakes his head, mumbles, "Crazy boys," and throws the booklet onto the couch.

He gets up, puts his cup of tea to his lips, and looks over to the Statue of Liberty, which seems to be hit at that very moment by a massive fireball… and falls over slowly. He spills his tea all over his shirt, and his eyes open up wide.

Harry pulls his camera out of his bag. Here is a much bigger story, this will make him famous. He presses the start button, but only "low battery" appears on the display. He throws the camera to the ground, just as he'd done with his phone before. He has no idea that he caused the perfect shot. He executed the Statue of Liberty!

Harry is a born loser. Aren't the journalists the real heroes of wars? Mostly not, but in this attack, Harry definitely played his part. And, as in any war, he never will be awarded either.

While I hug Brad, I see the balcony door of suite 788 open, and I quickly pull him into the room, where we see exactly what we've observed outside on the news channel inside. I change channels up and down, but there is only one picture: the Statue of Liberty on her knees, facing the ground. Various commentators are trying to describe what has happened, but nobody's got an explanation available, and the picture is stark and cold. There is no fire, and there are no flames. There is not even dust, just a nearly-fifty-metre Statue of Liberty on her knees, facing Manhattan, head down. By now the sky is full of helicopters, and more and more different impression are shown on the TV screen. Minutes later, an amateur movie shows the whole fall of the big lady, but there is still no explanation of how it might have happened.

A speaker of the white house denies any comment at this stage.

When I look down from the balcony, I can see hundreds of thousands of people streaming to the pier. I don't know it, but one of them is a very, very sad Harry. He's missed out on the chance of his lifetime.

If his camera had only been charged properly. Shame.

Then there is a vibration in my jeans. I check my phone. There is an SMS, and I open it. There are only three words from an unknown number: *Check your account.*

I show the message to Brad, before I sit at my laptop and open my internet banking,

It takes a while to load. I can imagine how busy the internet might be.

Brad keeps on watching the island, which is surrounded by navy and police boats, trying to keep civilians and media away. One never knows how dangerous the situation may be. I could tell them that nothing more is going to happen, but why should I? And who would believe me anyway?

There, my Thai internet banking opens up, but there is nothing new... Oh, there it pops up!

I rub my eyes, and now I can read it clearly: an amount of five million dollars was transferred into my account, from a production company in Los Angeles, United States. At the same time, the Thai bank sends me an email to confirm the transaction.

I cannot describe how I feel. This day was planned so differently, but now I am sitting in a cosy hotel room, watching from afar the result of three hundred old landmines and an huge, cast iron V8 engine, all put together using a nearly-forgotten formula. But the proof is here, right here in New York, and by now worldwide on TV screens. I can see Chinese, Russian, German, Italian commentators rushing over the screen, and it is not even an hour ago that my alarm clock rang. I join Brad outside on the balcony. It is unbelievable what has happened this year on September eleven, exactly ten years after the plane crashed into the World Trade Centre.

I pull Brad in and show him the bank statement. He screams, he shouts he jumps, and now I wake up. It is all over. We might not even have to run. It is all over, and we have five million dollars more than we had an hour ago! Yeeaaahhh! I call reception and extend our stay for another three days.

Then I receive another email. It is from Uncle Achmeth:

"Sorry we could not attend the party, but we are proud of you. I believe you should have received our gift by now?"

I go back to my bank statement, and piss myself laughing. The five in front of the six zeros has changed to a ten; there are ten million US dollars on my account now!

"Brraaadddddddd, we are rich! We made it, and I don't even feel bad about anything!"

At the same time, a New York City official announces on TV that no dead bodies have been found on, or around, Liberty Island, and that the police and army are still investigating how the "accident" could have happened.

I answer the mail to Uncle Achmeth with one word:

"Lovely!"

Pouring the last cognac from the mini-bar in my coffee, I realize what must have happened in the last hour. Firstly, someone must have dialled by mistake the number for the cell phone I had attached via electric capsule to our cannon. This person will most probably never know what he did, but he did it at the best possible moment! While I was staring from behind my binoculars, not believing what I saw and full of worries.

On the television, the first "specialists" are trying to reconstruct what happened to the statue to cause her to fall over on her knees. There is talk about the rough sea, and the strong winds of nearly twenty knots, blah, blah, blah. Because of how TNT is, there are no leftovers. I bet there is not a speck of fibre to be found from Walky; everything, including the heavy engine, got melted in the explosion of one and a half tonnes of TNT.

Brad can't stop watching over to the island. Then he hugs me, and he says, "German, you did it, you really did it. I asked you a few months ago at my campfire if you could really do it, and damn, you did it!

"Yes, WE did it, YOU, ME and Walky did it! My dear friend Brad, I was never sure if my calculation with the load would work out, but there was no one to ask for advice. Maybe half the load would have been enough, but you know, I also always order the biggest steak, in case the small portions are too small, so... well, I do well with that experience."

Now I spot Steven on his balcony. Damn it, he is the only one who is supposed to know what happened... and how... and by who. He only lifts his thumb, and in his other hand holds a glass of champagne! I take it as a sealed deal and return his toast. I am sure that there won't come any danger from his side; he could have warned the authorities after reading my story!

He is now owner of all rights to my book, and now, after he has transferred the five million dollars, he will most probably produce the movie, a movie of which he has witnessed, together with the author on balconies of Manhattan Hilton, the official end in reality. What a premiere! Lovely!

Brad asks, "What next?"

"Well, let's go down and join the crowd. Maybe we'll hear what really happened!" Smile... and it is time for room service... and the mini bar is empty.

Our job is done. I cannot believe it. Yes, our job is done. It is suddenly all over. The pressure, the nerves, the worries are gone. And, from the look of my bank statement, we will never have worries again. Lovely!

AN ACT OF GOD

The worries are somewhere else. They are now in the White House, and in the Pentagon. Their intelligence personnel are trying to investigate. Hundreds of officials meet and discuss what has happened. The president wants an explanation, and the citizens of the United States want an explanation from him. Well, the whole world wants to know!

I wonder which one he will bring up.

Please Mr. President, wake up, and don't come up with another war idea! Oh I hope he gets to read my story soonest!

I do not want to be in his pants today, or actually ever. All kinds of leaders and politicians who are in New York on invitation of the White House for the ten year memorial, step in front of a camera, but really do not know what to say. The picture of the Statue of Liberty on her knees is very impressive, and makes one speechless... as it was supposed to do!

No claims for responsibility for this event are received, authorities are in the dark.

On the other side, there are no victims or casualties either, only one big lady, who is on her knees, as if she were begging for mercy.

But how will the most powerful man in the world explain what happened, to his citizens? All members of the crisis meetings are helpless, or still speechless. There is no proof of any attack from the air or even from a submarine. The highest military officers cannot come up with an explanation. There is a huge crisis in the oval office. The highest general in command shakes his head and grumbles, "Only God knows!"

The president gives him his serious face. "So, this was an act of God? Is that what it is? Is that what I have to explain to our citizens and to the rest of the world?"

The president is upset and is losing his temper, which has never been witnessed before by his team. He leaves the conference room, slamming the door. Going back to his office he stares at his screens.

It is still the same picture as before: the Statue of Liberty on her knees, facing the ground!

We see the same picture on the big screen in downtown. Hundreds of people are standing around this public TV, waiting, as are billions of others worldwide, for an explanation. Then I hear someone screaming my name... but it can't be for me.

The voice, however, gets closer and closer, and now this voice screams, "William, you German bastard, now I've got you!" I turn my head to the little fat creature who has just called me a bastard, and ask him what he smoked this morning, while I put his shirt and jacket straight, trying to make him look a little bit more human.

"So, since you know my name, and where I am from, can I ask who you are?"

"I am Harry, and I have followed you from Mazar. I've been in Kenya and Mozambique. I believe you've got something bad in mind." Now he makes me smile, and I put my hand on his shoulder.

"You are a big adventurer, it seems. So, how can I help you, my friend?" I ask him.

Harry is so excited. He says that he knows about the credit card fraud and the mines, and that he'll brings me to court and to justice. I tell him that I paid back the amount that I took, together with high interest, this morning! He looks sceptical, and says that he tried to call me this morning shortly after five but couldn't get hold of me.

"Oh... was it you? You must have dialled the wrong number, but at least you did it at the best possible moment! Thank you for your support, you are not as useless as you look. But please, don't call again," and I push him back into the masses, while the first tears of laughter run from my eyes. Can I believe it? The press again. See how dangerous they are, when they put their finger into things which are not meant to be for them?

The President's personal assistant knocks anxiously on his private office door, and opens it. "Mr. President, there is someone who says he knows everything about the incident, but he only wants to speak to you alone, under four eyes!"

"Who is he? Where is he?"

"I believe you know this gentleman. It is Steven Spielberg!"

The President is shaking his head. "Oh no, not a moviemaker, even though I wish that this all would only be a movie. Okay, I'll give him three minutes, not a second more. Take him to my office.

So Steven Spielberg gets ushered under guard to the president's office, and is introduced. These two well-known personalities know each other only by reputation. They sit down, and then Steven starts talking.

"Mr. President, what happened this morning is as a result of a unique action by two relatively innocent young men!" The President can't work with that, and only reminds him that he's got two minutes left, and had better get on with a good explanation.

Then Steven pulls out the book of Williams' story, without front-page and contact details, and hands it over to the president.

"Please read the first three pages, and the last three. Please do so, and you will find the answer."

The president gives him a very sceptical look, but Steven tries to calm him down, opens the booklet for him and holds it to him to read. The president does, and he reads through the first three pages, and then he reads some more. Ten minutes... twenty minutes... nearly half an hour... Then he closes the book.

"Where did you get this?"

"Aeeheemm..." Steven grumbles. "It got delivered to my hotel!"
"It got delivered to your hotel?" the president repeats. "Anonymously, I presume?"
"That's correct," Mr. Spielberg admits.
The president keeps his face in his hands, not knowing what to say. There is a knock on his door, his personal assistant again, and she pressures the president, saying that his whole nation is waiting for his statement, and oh, by the way, there is no further news from the navy diver around the Liberty Island. All they found is a piece of fibre, most probably from a boat... and she hands a metre-long piece over to the president's desk. Unfortunately, Steven cannot grab a look at it, but it makes the President get up, and then he shows Steven to the door, asking his assistant to guide him out.
"Thank you very much, Mr. Spielberg. This conversation stays confidential?"
"Of course, sir!" Steven confirms.
After Steven has left, the president asks his assistant to send him the head of the New York City architects. He says that he has to see him immediately, that it is very important.
Luckily, Mr. Juan, the most senior architect, is close by, and the president has a five-minute talk to him, which looks from afar like he is giving an order, and the architect has nothing to say, other than "Yes, of course Mr. President". After the quick meeting in the corridor he disappears with fast steps.
Then the President sits behind his desk, keeping the piece of fibre board in his hand, he gets wet eyes, and keeps on checking all TV stations. It is always the same picture on each channel: the lady on her knees, head facing the ground. Only the broken down torch is moving in her right hand, like a lantern. He knows this picture is being seen around the world, on billions of screens, and every viewer is waiting for an explanation.
He grabs his phone with the other hand, and announces his speech will be held in twenty minutes, and leaves his office ten

minutes later, leaving behind a piece of a boat made out of fibre on his desk. On it is written: *Walk the Talk*!

We are still downtown, on a street, witnessing the crowds of people. We've got nothing to be scared of so far. In a huge shopping centre, we stop as the President appears on another big screen. It is now nearly ten o'clock in the morning; beer o'clock for me since nine!

The President of the United States of America starts his speech.

"My dear citizens of the United States of America.

What happened this morning to Liberty Island ten years, exactly to the day, after the horrible plane crash into the World Trade Centre on September eleven 2001, was NOT another terror attack!

I can tell you, and there is no doubt about it, this incident was not a terror attack to the United States of America by any suspicious group or as a result of any conflict from the past.

Yes, my fellow American people, it was not a terrorist attack that brought our Statue of Liberty to her knees. I can guarantee you that there is no foreign power involved. Plans for demolition and renovation were lying on my desk for a long time. This was just an accident in the long-planned renovation of the old statue. A mistake made in preparing for the demolition of the breakable old monument building, which was already life-threatening to its visitors, brought our potent and powerful symbol of liberty and freedom down.

As we promised ten years ago, we will make sure that something similar to the fatal plane crash into the Twin Towers will never happen again, and we made that promise to protect our country and people from any further attacks.

What happened today was purely an accident, or I might even call it an act of God. As time and strong weather conditions have worked on the statue over more than a hundred years, they have made her vulnerable and weak. Just as ten years of war with hardly any positive achievement has made us and our economy extremely weak. We have learned another lesson which we won't forget.

When I look at our economy, reputation and financial situation, which have been damaged during the last years, while we fought wars far away from our own soil, then I want to apologize to our American people, and to everybody else out there on this planet. Everybody can make mistakes, even the United States, and I also make mistakes. We cannot change what happened, and what we have done wrong in the past, but we can change what is going to happen in the future, and there shall be more together than against!"

He looks down at his notes, biting on his lips and taking a deep breath.

"When I saw this morning the pictures of our broken down Statue of Liberty, I could not believe what I saw. But obviously I had to, and I would just like to say it once more: not one victim or casualty is claimed.

"As I sat today in my office, and looked at the picture of the broken down Statue of Liberty on her knees, it made me think. I felt like I'd been given a message by the universe – there is just no other way I can describe it.

Ten years of war against something that cannot be beaten by weapons, and which also brought our country financially to its knees, should be over! Now it is time for change. Sometimes one needs to let go, and to close a chapter, and to bring things to an end, to start new! Let us be united again, stronger than ever before, because we can!"

"We cannot change what happened to our ancestors and victims of wars, but we can change what will happen to our children! With a percentage of the budget we used for the War against Terrorism we will establish a special unit to fight terrorism. In future we'll do it the same way that they operate: undercover, with best standards of equipment and trained intelligence, all highly confidential and only for personnel directly involved. There will be no media coverage, other than news announced by myself!"

"Never, ever, will civilians get in-between fire and fighting again, whether caused by American soldiers or our alliances!"

"We will only bring the people who are directly involved to justice, and will never, ever again make the peaceful people in their country suffer."

"We have made mistakes, but we will never make such mistakes again. Too much money has been spent for far too few results. Too many innocent people have been killed and lost family and friends."

"From now on we are going to spend more of the budget in our Country, on our soil, for our people, for our children's future, and we will have big results again, and earn respect from the rest of the world again. It will be hard work, but I know we can, together we can do it!

"And we will get off our knees again, and will keep our heads up and will be proud of what we do and what we achieve with a new America without wars!"

Then his assistant puts a note on his speaker desk. The President studies it quickly, rubs his face, and stands up straight to the audience again.

"This is a time of change, and to demonstrate the goodwill, the belief that we can change, and set higher and better new goals, according to the good, old, established laws from the days when the statue got built and was given to us as a symbol of liberty and freedom, peace and human rights in democracy, we start right here..." and he points over to the big screen behind him.

"The new statue of liberty and freedom!" He presents a picture of the new design, which makes the audience speechless and the press go mad. There is screaming, applause and flashlights of cameras for minutes. The audience gets off their seats.

The president continues with his introduction.

"Now the three-hundred-metre-high 'Lady' will hold a globe in her left hand, in which a two-hundred-seat restaurant and conference facilities will be." He turns around and shows the plans of the new Statue of Liberty.

"Six times taller, with four elevators, three restaurants, and a helipad on top, this is a new symbol for the new era of a new America. A new time has started, where we will focus more and better on our country, and our people, giving back what the last ten years has taken from us! We will get back our strength and the strong economy we once had, because we can!"

"To make it clear and avoid any misunderstanding: we will help with other international crises when our help is needed to establish a world freedom, but not with weapons and soldiers. We have learned that lesson from the past, and the errors of the past will never get repeated!

"I was not in power when the United States started the 'War against Terror', but today I have the power to end this war!

It is high time to stop. Let us **Walk the Talk...**

NO MORE WAR !"

~ The End ~

By William Kornfeld   Cape Town, September eleventh 2011

AUTHOR'S NOTE

Dear reader, thank you very much for reading my first book. Although English is not my first language, I am sure I've explained the story quite clearly, and that is what counts! It all stays exciting if the message finally reaches the person who is supposed to get it.

I started writing this when I **didn't** get the offered job in Afghanistan, but I had already prepared myself for a while to go there, and had put in lots of thoughts about how it might be. Then the day came when they shot Osama bin Laden, and my fantasy went wild, and I couldn't stop.

The original version I finished exactly on September eleven in 2011, just when President Barack Obama made the speech for the ten-year anniversary of the Twin Tower Terror attack of 2001. As I witnessed his speech, I had a feeling he didn't know what to say, and I wished for him that he had read my book before.

Then I wasted nearly a year with editing, corrections and even a longer translation into German, my mother tongue. Thanks to a few friends who supported me strongly with all of that. Nothing is ever perfect, but now is the time to just publish it, with no guarantee of success, just as I didn't have any guarantee with my Boat **Walky** in the book: no risk, no fun!

I gave the manuscript up front to some friends to read and check, so I enjoyed a lot of positive and negative criticism before. I learned that I didn't have enough dialogue, that my sentences were too long, and that I repeated some phrases too often. One of these is that bloody wars are useless; but this can't be said enough anyway! Oh, and that there were too many girl stories! Well, that's me! To much beer and whiskey? Well, that's me too! We just live differently here in Africa, close to the wilderness, surrounded by endless beautiful nature and sunshine.

We live harder, and more intensively, than in most of the civilised European countries!

Mostly I've described people who really exist, and I know them personally, although unfortunately not Harun and Uncle Achmeth;

this two are pure fiction. But the poor, gorgeous girl, Angelina, from Maputo fish market exists, and the boy Clifford – I helped him to sneak into to SA five years ago and he is a happy waiter here in the Western Cape, and supports his family in Mozambique with his income.

I must say, I had fun, and enjoyed putting down my life story in a different frame very much, and editing some of my lively fantasy.

But the main thing stays: That I've exposed some of the ridiculous situations in our politics around the world.

I believe strongly that it's **TIME TO WALK THE TALK!**

Now the political events, ruled by crazy dictators, are getting more and more bizarre, years after a Saddam Hussein got hanged, a Ghadaffi got killed and a Mubarak got locked away. The question is: what is going to happen with Assad from Syria? And who might be the next country leader that goes mad?

As I mentioned in my book, I believe more and more in the old tactic of putting up a demand on paper, as Marshall John Wayne did in the good old days: Wanted 10Mil$ Reward! There are still enough crazy head hunters out in this world to do jobs like that, with less damage than an army, and without killing civilians.

Now to your question: would a self-built bomb like ours, using old mines, actually work?

Well, that's as uncertain as my question about how many books I might sell, if the Statue of Liberty goes on her knees tomorrow!

Let's stay in touch. I hope to see you soon in the cinema... or on a farm in Africa!

Regards from the most beautiful end of the World,

Cape Town, South Africa
William Kornfeld
william.kornfeld@yahoo.com

www.ingramcontent.com/pod-product-compliance
Lightning Source LLC
Chambersburg PA
CBHW071500040426
42444CB00008B/1430